VIBRATIONAL ASTROLOGY STUDY GUIDE

~ Module One ~

....

Association of
Vibrational Astrologers

Vibrational Astrology Study Guide Module One
Copyright by The Avalon School of Astrology, Inc.

All rights reserved. This book or any portion thereof may not be reproduced or used in any manner whatsoever without the express written permission of the publisher. Printed in the United States of America.

For information contact:
Association of Vibrational Astrologers
The Avalon School of Astrology, Inc.
6212 NW 43rd Street, Suite B
Gainesville, FL 32653
USA
http://www.astrovibe.org

Book design by Diane Ammons
Cover design by Starlene Breiter
All chart wheels and reports used in this module were created from Sirius 3.0 Astrology Software with permission of Cosmic Patterns Software.

ISBN: 978-1-7377403-4-6

First Edition: November 2021

Copyright © The Avalon School of Astrology, Inc.

*This study guide is dedicated to David Cochrane,
who has expanded the understanding of harmonics/vibrations through his
scientific research.*

Association of Vibrational Astrologers (AVA) Board:　　Diane Ammons
Linda Berry
Starlene Breiter
Fei Cochrane
Heather Curtis

The Association of Vibrational Astrologers (AVA) Board wishes to thank those who have contributed their time and energy in the creation of the Vibrational Astrology Study Guides.

Study Guide Committee, Module One
Diane Ammons, Chair
Linda Berry, Technical Consultant
Gale Cox, Wordsmithing/Design Consultant
Sharon Leopardi, Technical Consultant
Warren Peake, Wordsmithing/Design Consultant
Jackie Speen, Wordsmithing/Design Consultant

Additional Support
Starlene Breiter, Cover Design
Fei Cochrane, Proofreading Consultant
David Cochrane, Technical Editor

We sincerely wish to thank and acknowledge David and Fei Cochrane for their contributions, time, and support in this Study Guide project. David Cochrane has reviewed and approved the information and its presentation in the Study Guide, Module One.

Vibrational Astrology Study Guide Overview

This Study Guide contains a summary of the important topics required to interpret an astrology chart using the methodology taught In Vibrational Astrology. This is NOT a textbook and is intended to accompany training with a certified Vibrational Astrology Instructor. It is also intended as a reference source for a review of various topics related to VA.

The Study Guide is divided into four (4) modules covering the basic required knowledge for a VA astrologer.

Module One: How to Read an Astrology Chart Using VA
Module Two: VA Vibrations, Aspects, Advanced Midpoints, Signs, House System Models
Module Three: Forecasting, Relocation, Compatibility, Astronomy for Astrologers
Module Four: Research & Advanced Topics

It is highly recommended that the VA student begins with Module One in their study since the basic concepts of VA are described in that module. Each module builds on the information in the preceding module.

The Study Guide is also intended as a workbook. For that reason, blank spaces have been provided at the bottom of many pages and at the end of chapters for notetaking in classes, lectures, and/or videos. Vibrational Astrology is dynamic and still developing as more research is performed.

MODULE 1
How to Read an Astrology Chart Using VA

CONTENTS

"Harmonic" and "Vibration" are synonymous throughout this document.

Chapter 1: What is Vibrational Astrology?...1

    A. Brief History of Vibrational Astrology.......................................1
    B. The Basic Mechanics of Vibrational Astrology......................3
    C. An Evidence-based Approach to Astrology............................4
    D. Books & Videos...7

Chapter 2: Energy Processes & Behavioral Symptoms of Planets/Combinations...9

    A. Energy Processes and Behavior Symptoms of Planets.............9
    B. Energy Processes and Behavior Symptoms of Planetary Combinations..15
    C. Summary: Energy Processes of Planets/Combinations............31
    D. Books & Videos..36

Chapter 3: Aspects and Orbs...39

    A. Aspect Glyphs..39
    B. Ptolemaic Aspects...40
    C. Non-Ptolemaic Aspects..44
    D. VA Aspect Interpretation..47
    E. Proportional Orbs in Vibrational Charts...................................49
    F. Aspect Rules for Vibrational Charts..50
    G. Active and Inactive Aspect Circuits..52
    H. Aspect Patterns in VA..54
    I. Aspect Grids...61
    J. Summary: Aspects and Orbs...62
    K. Books & Videos...67

Chapter 4: VA Vibration Interpretations (1-13) 69

    A. Introduction..69
    B. The First 13 Vibrations.................................69
    C. Summary: VA Vibration Energy Processes & Behaviors (1-13)..77
    D. Books & Videos..80

Chapter 5: Basic VA Chart Interpretation..........................83

    A. What is a Vibrational (Harmonic) Chart?...............83
    B. Proportional Orbs and Aspect Color Settings........84
    C. Midpoint Patterns...85
        1. Midpoint Settings in VA..........................85
        2. Evaluating Midpoint Orbs.......................87
        3. Midpoints..88
        4. Isotraps...94
        5. Midpoint Isotraps................................100
    D. How to Read an Astrology Chart Using VA.......104
        1. Confirm the Birth Information & Source.....104
        2. Natal Chart...104
        3. Midpoint Patterns................................105
        4. Harmonic Listing #8.............................105
        5. Harmonic Listing #1.............................107
        6. Vibrations for Beginning Astrological Screening.........108
        7. Aspect Pattern Review........................109
    E. Summary: Basic VA Chart Interpretation..........111
    F. Books & Videos..117

Summary Compendium..119

Glossary of Terms...143

Index...149

Vibrational Astrology Study Guide Module One

Chapter 1: What Is Vibrational Astrology?

A. Brief History of Astrology
B. The Basic Mechanics of Vibrational Astrology
C. An Evidence-based Approach to Astrology
D. Books & Videos

A. Brief History of Vibrational Astrology

The earliest records of planetary and celestial observations appear as markings on bones and cave walls which show lunar cycles as early as 25,000 years ago.

By the 2nd millennium BCE, an organized system of astrology had been developed in Babylonia. If there were well-developed systems of astrology before this time, details of them have been lost. In the 6th century BCE, Greek philosopher and mathematician, Pythagoras, suggested a relationship between the movement of planets and musical theory. The mathematical intervals between the movement of planets produce a vibration or sound that we do not hear but respond to. This became known as *musica universalis* or "Music of the Spheres".

The oldest birth charts discovered are from the 5th century BCE in Mesopotamia. By 200 BCE, Hellenistic astrology or "horoscopic astrology" was being practiced in and around the Mediterranean region, especially in Egypt.

During this same period, Claudius Ptolemy (100-170 CE), referred to as the most famous of Greek astrologers, wrote his book, "Tetrabiblios". "Tetrabiblios" laid the basis for the Western astrological tradition. To this day, the basic five (5) astrological aspects in Western Astrology are referred to as Ptolemaic aspects. Ptolemy's writing included references to the "Music of the Spheres". This connected the harmonic, a mathematical concept, to the motion of the planets and our response to that movement.

Hellenistic astrology thrived in Europe until around the 7th century CE when Europe entered the Middle Ages. Individuals in the Islamic Empire continued their development into the 13th century CE.

By around the 13th century CE, Europe again became a developmental influence in astrology. Johannes Kepler (1571-1630), a German mathematician,

Copyright © The Avalon School of Astrology, Inc. All Rights Reserved
All chart wheels and reports used in this module are created from Sirius 3.0 with permission from Cosmic Patterns Software.

astronomer, and astrologer, is best known for his laws of planetary motion. Using his Third Planetary Law, Kepler studied the movements of the planets and

their relationships as vibrations or musical intervals. He also introduced the concept and importance of minor aspects in the tradition of Western astrology.

The Enlightenment or "Age of Reason" from 1685-1815 radically reoriented European politics, science, and communications. During this period, the rise of science pushed astrology to the side. In the late 1700s and 1800s, astrology reached its lowest point in popularity.

From the late 1800s to 1940, there was a theosophical revival of astrology. During this period, Alan Leo (1860-1917), a British astrologer and theosophist, developed an astrological system that is close to what we use today.

In 1928, Alfred Witte (1878-1941) first published his research on astrological midpoints and a 90° dial (4th harmonic) was developed by the Hamburg School of Astrology. In 1941, Reinhold Ebertin (1901-1988) adapted this extensive research as the foundation of his School of Cosmobiology. Ebertin continued to promote astrological research working on medical applications of astrology.

In 1976, John Addey (1920-1982), described his system of astrology, which he called "harmonic astrology". John Addey recognized that the twelvefold system of aspects was incomplete. He saw that the twelvefold system of aspects included cycles 2, 3, 4, 6, and 12 but did not include the cycles of 5, 7, 8, 9, 10, 11, or cycles greater than 12. The tools of astrology had to be improved. The search for some way of understanding these additional cycles led to the formulation of his theory of harmonics. Addey's empirical research confirmed his ideas.

In the late 20th and early 21st century, David Cochrane expanded the understanding of harmonics through scientific research. Using Extreme Case Sampling, Cochrane identified the core functions of vibrations 1 through 32. In addition, he more clearly identified the basic core functions of planets and signs. Cochrane continues to coordinate research into higher vibrations and their significance in the life of the individual.

We are living in a time of expanded awareness and theoretical physics is showing that vibration is a fundamental force. Vibrational Astrology is becoming part of this greater understanding.

B. The Basic Mechanics of Vibrational Astrology

Imagine the face of a Big Old Watch. Now, lift the face off the watch and see under it. Below lies a detailed arrangement of multiple wheels whirling around. Looking inside the watch gives you a new world of understanding of how the watch keeps time. Vibrational Astrology does this very thing, it opens the natal chart showing all the beautiful workings hidden inside.

Aspects are represented as divisions of the 360° wheel and every aspect is a vibration. For example, a square is 90 degrees, which is 1/4th of the 360° astrological chart. While 1/4th is a square aspect, it can also be represented as a vibration, the 4-Vibration. We can convert the chart into the 4-Vibration by multiplying all the planetary locations in the natal chart by 4 and converting the planetary positions to 360° notation. All vibrational charts are generated through this simple multiplication process. Therefore, vibrational charts can go to infinity. VA continues to explore the limits of our human capacity to sense these vibrations.

Vibrational Astrology is developing a greater understanding of how aspects work in various vibrations. Aspects in vibrational charts represent natal planetary relationships that are resonating at higher frequencies. When the base aspects appear, a resonance is active. The base aspects are Conjunction(1), Opposition(2), Trine(3), Square(4), Sextile(6), Semisquare & Sesquiquadrate (8), and Semisextile & Quincunx(12). Vibrational Charts are showing the character of these resonating frequencies that come from the natal chart. There are many additional aspects formed by the planets in the natal chart. All the aspects in the source or natal chart are equally important and influential in the generation and interpretation of vibrational charts. This expands and deepens the astrological understanding of planetary relationships and their effects on people.

Aspect structures involving three or more planets are required to form a vibrational energy circuit. Simple rules apply for identifying and reading these configurations, combining the meaning of the vibration with the meanings of the planets.

Through extreme case sampling, VA researchers led by David Cochrane have uncovered many of the meanings of the vibrations. This research identifies key issues, talents, and potential challenges to look for. VA has been successful in identifying consistent astrological patterns in the charts of musicians, athletes, and entertainers. Most importantly, using Vibrational Astrology, the astrologer is better able to quickly identify key characteristics and specific behaviors to aid their clients. VA brings a new level of depth to our understanding of astrology and how it relates to individual human experiences.

Research into methods of interpreting higher vibrations is ongoing. By utilizing Kepler and Sirius Astrology software we can see the many aspects that are not easily recognized in the natal chart and interpret them effectively.

C. An Evidence-based Approach to Astrology

In the 1960s and 1970s, interest in the science of astrology gained prominence within the astrological community. Most astrological evidence was collected through "convenience sampling" and "anecdotal evidence". The formal research studies that were conducted were heavily criticized by Geoffrey Dean in his very influential book "Recent Advances in Natal Astrology". Many critics concluded that empirical research into astrology produced little evidence to support astrology. Geoffrey Cornelius in his book, "The Moment of Astrology", suggests, at the time of its publication, astrologers have not achieved substantial evidence supporting the field of astrology as a studied science. Efforts had not produced definitive or replicable measurable effects. By the late 1970s and early 1980s, the search for scientific proof of astrology's usefulness diminished.

In the 1970-80s, David Cochrane began using "extreme case sampling" to remove the selection bias in viewing astrological charts. This is one of the research methods within the category of "intensity case sampling" used by research methods experts.

The core ideas in VA have research support and are part of an evidence-based approach that has applied the very rigorous standards in the hard sciences. In some of the research, such as the bipolar disorder research conducted by Gisele Terry and David Cochrane, the Gold Research by Linda Berry and David Cochrane, the extraversion-introversion research by Dr. David Fink and David Cochrane, the very positive results suggest that scientific research in astrology can produce definitive and unambiguous support for astrology, but more replications of the studies are needed before this very high level of confidence is achieved.

The theoretical framework of VA utilizes the astrological variables such as aspects, zodiac signs, placement of houses, etc. It is understood within a context that is consistent with ideas in quantum physics such as the fundamental importance of Space, structures within Space, the process of Dimension Reduction, the fundamentals of Spin, Mass, and Charge, and the importance of mathematical modeling utilizing prime numbers and Pisano periods.

There are 4 levels of concepts that VA Astrologers recognize, and each of these levels generates a different level of confidence in its concepts that is based on how the concepts are confirmed at that level.

"Level I" VA - Level I is the concepts and techniques that are well-researched and are confirmed with a controlled research study as well as through consultations and chart analysis. Examples of controlled research are extreme case sampling studies and statistical tests that compare groups. These concepts and techniques are the core of Vibrational Astrology. Examples of Level I concepts are aspect interpretations up to the vibrations that have been evaluated in extreme case studies, midpoints, and interpretation of zodiac signs.

"Level II" VA - Level II techniques are based on ideas that are consistent with Vibrational Astrology theory and research and have been used extensively by some Certified Vibrational Astrologers. These specific ideas have not yet been confirmed in controlled research studies but some of the components of these ideas are Level I concepts and techniques. Examples of Level II VA concepts would be House Systems and interpretation of planets in Houses.

"Level III" VA - Level III techniques are based on ideas that are consistent with vibrational theory and research and have NOT been used extensively by most Certified Vibrational Astrologers. These ideas have also not yet been confirmed in controlled research studies. Examples of Level III VA concepts would be the importance of solar arcs to natal midpoint structures.

"**Non-VA:** - Non-VA includes techniques and concepts that are not derived from VA Theory and have not been integrated into VA.

There are astrological techniques that do not fit easily into these 3 levels. For example, fixed stars are a Level 3 idea that one could argue there is nothing in fundamental VA theory that suggests that they should work, but on the other hand, one could argue that VA detects patterns in the visible and nearly visible sky and fixed stars would very likely be important from the VA theoretical framework.

In Level One, controlled studies are performed in which some of the weaknesses of anecdotal evidence are removed. For example, selection bias may be removed by using a computer procedure where charts are selected based on their strength in a specified set of characteristics rather than having the researcher select the charts and possibly exert either an unconscious or conscious influence on which charts are used in the study. In a controlled research study using a software program with a large database, people can be selected based on which ones have the greatest strength in specific astrological variables. Thus, selection bias is removed. If one finds a common theme that fits the pre-research interpretation of those specific astrological variables, then one MIGHT have an accurate interpretation. If the pre-research interpretation does NOT fit the strongest chart data, then that interpretation is almost certainly wrong! This method is simple and scientifically recognized. Working to remove selection bias using extreme case sampling, builds a body of empirical data that improves the accuracy of astrological interpretations.

D. Books & Videos

Books

Berry, Linda & Cochrane, David, *Vibrational Astrology, Interpreting Aspects,* Gainesville: Cosmic Patterns Software, inc., 2016. (Order through http://www.Lulu.com)

Cochrane, David, *Vibrational Astrology, the Essentials,* Gainesville, Florida: Cosmic Patterns Software, Inc, 2021

Videos

A. Brief History of Astrology -
Astrology Tutorial Videos by David Cochrane
      Https://www.astrologydc.com
The History of Astrology from the Earliest Beginnings to Today and The Future of Astrology
The Harmonic Astrology of Claudius Ptolemy
The Music of the Spheres and Harmonic Astrology: An Ancient Tradition
Astrology of the Ottoman Empire: New Findings by Oner Doser

B. The Basic Mechanics of Vibrational (Harmonic) Astrology
Astrology Tutorial Videos by David Cochrane
      Https://www.astrologydc.com
Theory of Astrology, Theoretical Frameworks
How Astrology Works: A New Theoretical Framework

C. An Evidence-Based Approach to Astrology
Astrology Tutorial Videos by David Cochrane
      Https://www.astrologydc.com
Astrology Research: How to do it
What is Evidence-Based Astrology
Extreme Case Sampling: The Fast Path to Understanding Astrology
The *Research Revolution* in Astrology
Introduction to Astrology Research Using Kepler or Sirius
Astrology Research: Evaluating Your Findings

Notes

CHAPTER 2: Energy Processes & Behavioral Symptoms of Planets/Combinations

A. Energy Processes & Behavior Symptoms of Planets
B. Energy Processes & Behavior Symptoms of Planetary Combinations
C. Summary: Energy Processes of Planets/Combinations
D. Books & Videos

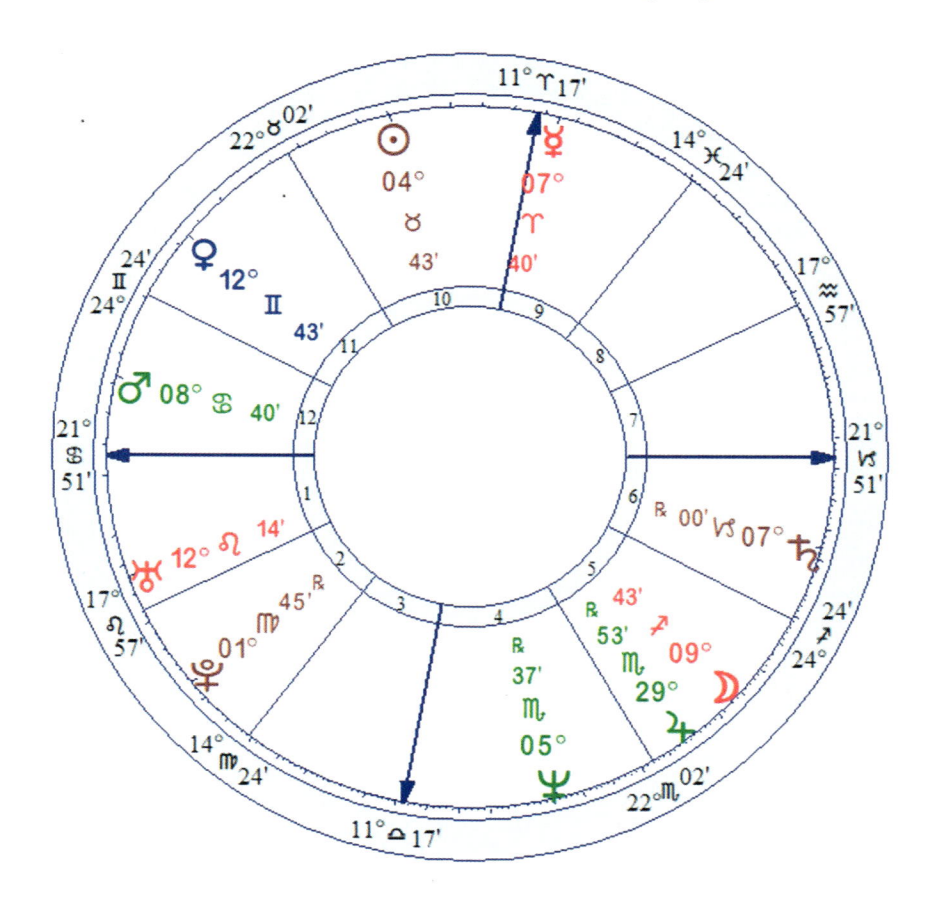

A. Energy Processes & Behavior Symptoms of Planets

Sun	☉	Mars	♂	Uranus	♅
Moon	☽	Jupiter	♃	Neptune	♆
Mercury	☿	Saturn	♄	Pluto	♇ or P
Venus	♀				

Energy Processes & Behavior Symptoms of Planets/Combinations

In Vibrational Astrology (VA), each planet is seen as providing its specific purpose, function, and motivation. Many of the behavior patterns that each of us experience and express are built into the fabric of the Universe at the time of our birth. They are not just in our genetic code. The planets express or regulate these primary and essential parts of us. This idea helps explain the results of controlled research studies better than describing the astrological impact of planets as fundamentally archetypal. The archetypal stories and images that guide people's lives are born out of the fundamental forces, personal experiences, and decisions that people make.

Planets are understood to each have a simple basic energy. These energies are combined or linked by the planetary aspects. Aspects containing the Inner planets, Sun, Moon, Mercury, Venus, Mars, generate behaviors that one identifies with, feeling as if one is the source of those thought processes, feelings, attractions, motivations, etc.

An aspect circuit consisting solely of planets beyond Mars (Jupiter, Saturn, Uranus, Neptune, Pluto) results in an experience that feels as if it is coming from outside. Of the 45 pairs of planets formed using Sun through Pluto, only ten (10) pairs are composed entirely of impersonal planets. These impersonal aspect patterns can still be strong determiners of behavior. If there are one or more inner planets involved with the outer planets, the behavior will be experienced as personal.

Following are VA interpretations of planets showing both the energy processes and the behavioral symptoms ascribed to each planet as a result of research in which the selection bias has been removed. (Extreme Case Sampling)

Sun:

Energy Process: The Sun connects us to the current moment and regulates what we are conscious of at any given time.

Discussion: The Sun and Moon regulate our relationship to time. Without a connection to time, there is no conscious awareness. The way we experience being conscious is to notice what is happening in the current moment. We are conscious of the parts of the present reality that the Sun is shining its light on. Our experience of time is to feel it as a long string that stretches into the distant past, through the current moment, and into the future. This is the process hidden behind how we experience the Sun astrologically.

Behavioral Symptoms: In the astrology chart the Sun brings us awareness of the current moment, and thus the Sun determines what the clear and present reality is. The effect of the Sun is to bring simple and straightforward attention to what is happening around us. Without the Sun we are not anchored to the "now" We need this anchor to experience consciousness. The net effect of the Sun in our lives is very simple: an aspect of another planet to the Sun brings that planet into our conscious daily life. That planet is highlighted in our daily awareness and is important in our daily activities and thus may be evident in a person's career. There is nothing imaginary about the Sun, nothing intuitive or psychic, nothing mental or emotional. It is the light of day shining in our lives in the here and now.

Moon:

Energy Process: The Moon brings the past into the present, regulating what elements of the past we are aware of.

Discussion: Without the Moon all the experiences in the present moment, that the Sun makes available to us, would immediately disappear from awareness. It regulates what the subconscious transmits to the conscious mind. The Moon retains awareness of previous experiences, and this is the source of memory, habits, and anything else that is connected to the past.

Behavioral Symptoms: Common expressions of the Moon are an interest in history, psychology, anthropology, genealogy, culture, and tradition. The Moon is about the things that develop over time including memory, soul, habits, instincts, moods, and connection to ancestry and possibly to past lives. The Moon operates based on the past. The person is guided by past experiences stored in their memory. In traumatic situations, these memories can have intense energy stored in them. These memories shape our emotional responses and attitudes in the present and inform our intuitions. This creates instinctual habits connecting us to our early life, ancestry, and perhaps to past lives.

Energy Processes & Behavior Symptoms of Planets/Combinations

<u>Note: The Sun comprises over 99% of the mass of the Solar System, and the Sun and Moon appear to be the same size to our eyes. Although the Sun is massive and sustains life on our planet, it is not as dominant in the astrological interpretation as it is in our physical lives. The Sun as our daily attention is like the lens through which we observe everything, and it is not generally noticed. The Moon is whether we are comfortable or not and how we feel about the experiences we are having. The Sun and Moon make consciousness possible and form the stage on which life happens. The Dance of Life is expressed by the planets which are on the stage made possible by the Sun and Moon.</u>

Mercury:

Energy Process: Mercury makes mental connections and communicates; sees relationships and associations, notices and compares similarities and differences.

Behavioral Symptoms: Mercury is engaged in the formulation of thoughts based on evaluation and contrast of many mental threads forming them into a cohesive, organized whole. The extremely fast associations and comparisons that Mercury makes, build to form ideas that the person considers and communicates to others. Mercury affects one's IQ.

Venus:

Energy Process: Venus regulates the magnetic power of attraction to beauty.

Behavioral Symptoms: Beauty is inherently attractive, and Venus quickly and instinctively formulates a sense of how beautiful and attractive something is. Venus identifies what we are attracted to and what we attract, and this generates a feeling. This feeling is powerful and goes beyond physical appearances. The power of attraction can be perceived with the mind or any of our senses: sound, sight, smell, touch, taste, and in the body's physical movements. It is a fundamental energetic principle of the universe. Venus quickly assesses proportion, symmetry, color combinations, patterns, harmonies, and other factors. This is the intelligence in Venus that organically and intuitively senses the details of the attraction. There are rules for this based on mathematics that describe this process, but Venus does not analyze it intellectually; it intuitively senses and responds to it. We are attracted to or repelled by what we encounter, and Venus regulates this process.

Mars:
Energy Process: Mars is the dynamic force needed to achieve the drive to reach a goal.
Behavioral Symptoms: Mars is energy in action. It is the impulse needed to achieve a goal. Mars brings vitality to life and shows us life is not static. It is built into the nature of life, into the nature of reality that life is dynamic, propelling us forward and giving a sense of achievement. This is the force of Mars. It does not judge positive or negative, it just needs to take action, and the nature of that action is shaped by its relationship to other planets. Frustration and anger may occur if the action of Mars is interrupted or stymied.

Jupiter:
Energy Process: Jupiter is the energy force that grows and expands. Without Jupiter, there is no growth.
Behavioral Symptoms: Jupiter makes things bigger without changing their basic nature or structure. Jupiter's process of expansion generates a sense of optimism, openness, and inclusiveness. Thus, it creates diversity and generates a feeling of optimism. Jupiter, by itself, can over-expand and collapse if not tempered by other planets.

Saturn:
Energy Process: Saturn is the energy force that removes all that is superficial to discover the essence, the foundations, the essential core.
Behavioral Symptoms: Saturn evaluates a construct or pattern to establish what is fundamentally essential and removes everything else. What is essential is whatever is necessary for that construct or pattern to be sustained. Saturn's focus is on that which has lasting value and stands the test of time (that which lasts past death). Saturn can be demanding and is often experienced as a taskmaster.

Energy Processes & Behavior Symptoms of Planets/Combinations

Uranus:
Energy Process: Uranus is the energy force that acts in the current moment without regard for the past or future.
Behavioral Symptoms: Each moment in time is composed of waves of energy and Uranus subconsciously experiences the waves of energy of the current moment and expresses it spontaneously. Uranus has no interest in the past or the future, not what happened an hour ago, nor what will happen an hour from now. The focus is on this moment, right now. Energy flows in waves and Uranus puts us on the wave at the current moment. Uranus is spontaneous, it subconsciously experiences the current wave of energy and improvises. Therefore, it is often associated with sports, music, and humor, anything that demands being in the moment. It is not inherently rebellious. It just wants to be in the moment. It does not care about rules and regulations or consequences. If restricted, rebellion or chaotic behavior is likely. When it is free to express itself, it is not chaotic. Rather it allows us to experience the reality of each moment.

Neptune:
Energy Process: Neptune is the force of attraction to dreams, visions, ideals.
Behavioral Symptoms: Neptune enlightens and enhances, bringing a sense of wonder and magic to life's dreams, visions, and ideals. Neptune inclines us to follow our dream. It ignites our imagination, vision, or sense of wonder and awe. Neptune's energy perceives life as magical, special, and intoxicating. It inspires life, making it magical to the person and therefore adding meaning to his or her life. Neptune is not necessarily spiritual or overly idealistic. Whatever the dream may be, money, animals, travel, food, literature, etc., Neptune energizes it, drawing us to it and it to us. Neptune is lifting us out of the mundane or boring. It cannot tolerate a life without wonder and vision. The planets connected with Neptune indicate the nature of the dream, vision, ideal, or idea that is so wonderful, magical, glamorous.

Pluto:
Energy Process: Pluto is energy from the deep past that expresses itself forcefully as compulsiveness or even obsession.
Behavioral Symptoms: Pluto, as part of any planetary pattern, makes the pattern compulsive and obsessive, generating an intensity that goes beyond logic or reasoning. It is a deeply rooted irrational force and tends to be cyclical, turning on and off. Pluto does not modify the meaning of the patterns it works in, rather it adds emphasis, intensity, and, sometimes, extreme focus to that planetary pattern. In a strong pattern, the compulsive obsessive nature of Pluto will manifest in compelling and powerful behaviors.

Vibrational Astrology Study Guide Module One

B. Energy Processes & Behavior Symptoms of Planetary Combinations

In VA we interpret planetary circuits consisting of three or more planets following strict guidelines. We do not usually interpret two planet patterns. However, in this section, two planet aspect interpretations are provided as a foundation for the interpretation of larger patterns. Even though these interpretations may seem limited, they will work consistently when the two planets are part of a circuit as described in Chapter 3.

SUN

Sun-Moon –
Energy Process: Appreciates how the past is the basis or foundation of the present bringing the hidden or shadowed into the light of the present
Behavioral Symptoms: Sun-Moon is our feelings, mood, and attitude in this present moment. It is our memories of the past influencing everything we do in the present moment. Sun-Moon has an interest in how history, heritage, and the environment are reflected in the present. This often results in an interest in subjects such as history and psychology.

Sun-Mercury –
Energy Process: Brings clear and present thought and communication
Behavioral Symptoms: Sun-Mercury will speak and write in a clear, upfront way. It wants to evaluate what is, what needs to be done and how to do it. It does not want to speculate or go deeply under the surface into causes. It just wants to talk about what is here and how to think about it right now.

Energy Processes & Behavior Symptoms of Planets/Combinations

Sun-Venus –
Energy Process: A clear and present beauty
Behavioral Symptoms: Sun-Venus brings an appreciation or affinity for clear, simple beauty. It calls attention to the beauty of symmetry, a pattern, a sound, etc. as if a light were shined on it. It is clear and straightforward with no drama, and nothing hidden, subtle, mystical, or esoteric.

Sun-Mars –
Energy Process: A clear and present force to achieve, a drive to do something tangible, something real
Behavioral Symptoms: Sun-Mars has a love of action and a desire to get things done, not in the future, but right now. It is impatient to get something done. It is not about planning but doing it.

Sun-Jupiter –
Energy Process: A clear and present ongoing growth and expansion
Behavioral Symptoms: Sun-Jupiter does not want to be limited by current circumstances. It has a desire to reach out, explore, socialize, or expand. This person wants to grow beyond the environment they grew up in.

Sun-Saturn –
Energy Process: A clear and present desire to get rid of everything that is not essential
Behavioral Symptoms: Sun-Saturn focuses on what is important, the essential elements of the current situation. It will eliminate what is unnecessary with no-nonsense practical efficiency. It filters out glamour, ostentatiousness, and the superfluous. It has a desire to get to something that is real and has lasting purpose and meaning. The interest is in maintaining that which has long-term significance. This person is responsible and aware of the consequences of his or her actions.

Vibrational Astrology Study Guide Module One

Sun-Uranus –

Energy Process: Attunes to the waves and cycles of the moment expressing them as a clear and present spontaneity

Behavioral Symptoms: Sun-Uranus is in the current moment. The energy is quick to respond, quick to laugh, and is alert and lively. This combination is spontaneous and can easily improvise in the moment. It can also result in frustration and rebellion when blocked.

Sun-Neptune –

Energy Process: Brings a clear and present sense of attraction to the wonder and magic of dreams, visions, and ideals

Behavioral Symptoms: There is a child-like optimism, a feeling of fascination, wonder, and magic. Sun-Neptune needs to live life this way. Life must have magic. It cannot stand to live in a mundane world. With Sun-Neptune, there are special songs, places, people, etc. and simple everyday experiences can be full of wonder. Life does not have to be exotic to be magical.

Sun-Pluto –

Energy Process: Makes daily life compulsive and obsessive

Behavioral Symptoms: Sun-Pluto lives a life of passion and mission. It is driven by an uncompromising sense that life is a commitment to a destiny or purpose. It operates from instinct and passion and cannot always do things based on logic and reason.

Energy Processes & Behavior Symptoms of Planets/Combinations

MOON

Moon-Mercury –
Energy Process: Thinking about the past and how the past influences the present
Behavioral Symptoms: Moon-Mercury is easy to talk to because it understands people, their history, and heritage. It has strong intuitions about how an individual's past is influencing the way he or she operates in the present. Moon-Mercury finds it easy to see how events connect with moods and feelings, making for excellent counselors. These individuals are likely to be interested in history, psychology, and anthropology, subjects that study how the past affects the present.

Moon-Venus –
Energy Process: Attraction to the beauty of the past
Behavioral Symptoms: Moon-Venus is a soulful depth found in the past, in history, in a long, rich heritage, and in family traditions. It is devoted to home and family, especially the mother. Moon-Venus is attracted to interactions and experiences that admire and highlight the past and finds history rich with meaning and soul. There is comfort in living surrounded by items reflecting the past.

Moon-Mars –
Energy Process: Enjoys the feeling of accomplishment and is always seeking to improve its skills
Behavioral Symptoms: Moon-Mars has a heightened emotional drive to be active, to achieve, to strive for goals. Its actions are often inspired by observing others. There is a desire to test one's resolve, to push the edge. Moon-Mars is not idle. It values a good competition, making it a gracious winner or loser. It is often critical of people who are lazy or make excuses. Moon-Mars feels that people should be motivated, get energized, and not be afraid of life's challenges.

Copyright © The Avalon School of Astrology, Inc. All Rights Reserved
All chart wheels and reports used in this module are created from Sirius 3.0 with permission from Cosmic Patterns Software.

Moon-Jupiter –

Energy Process: Has expansive moods and enjoys an open atmosphere
Behavioral Symptoms: Moon-Jupiter is open and welcoming. It values an inclusive and expansive atmosphere and is interested in different perspectives and beliefs coming from multiple historical narratives and cultural backgrounds. It desires interactions that cultivate feelings of openness, welcoming all perspectives, histories, and viewpoints, thus enabling growth into a larger, more interesting life.

Moon-Saturn –

Energy Process: Has a need for isolation that quiets the emotions enabling one to perceive deep essential long-lasting truths
Behavioral Symptoms: Moon-Saturn is introverted and needs solitude. It requires quiet to get beyond the frivolous and connect with what is beneath appearances. Moon-Saturn focuses on the core essence of reality. It is looking for a soul connection with others seeking those who are interested in deep relationships. Its relationships are based on sincerity and authenticity. Moon-Saturn is deeply sincere, and it looks beneath the surface to sense if the other person is as well. It has little need for or interest in superficial interactions.

Moon-Uranus –

Energy Process: Needs to feel free and unrestricted by expectations and consequences
Behavioral Symptoms: Moon-Uranus needs to laugh, breathe, and act freely and spontaneously. It is quick to feel restricted by rigid or formal social norms or any limiting environmental pressures. It desires the feeling of spontaneous, in-the-moment, impulsive expression. Moon-Uranus is comfortable with traditions that are alive and evolving right now. It is very sensitive to any attempt to restrict and limit its freedom of expression. If restricted, it may become rebellious.

Energy Processes & Behavior Symptoms of Planets/Combinations

Moon-Neptune –

Energy Process: Sensitive to the atmosphere and mood
Behavioral Symptoms: Moon-Neptune is a gentle stimulation of the senses. It is acutely sensitive and responsive to the surrounding atmosphere, having an appreciation for the effect of candles, soft music, and a sensitivity to color, texture, light, smell, etc. The sensitivity to mood can bring an unconscious selection of atmospheres that feel right or comfortable. Stories, myths, music, and culture can instill a sense of magic and excitement. Moon-Neptune avoids a noisy or chaotic atmosphere. Being sensitive and responsive to the atmosphere, it has a keen ability to arrange a space to match the mood that is desired. This attention to spatial patterning can develop into talent and expertise.

Moon-Pluto –

Energy Process: Powerful concentrations of past feelings erupt forcefully into the present
Behavioral Symptoms: Moon-Pluto brings the potential for powerful eruptions of feelings coming from deep within. These eruptions often are not controllable. One needs to grab hold and accept that all you can do is hang on for the ride. There is the potential of separating yourself from other people if this happens. Moon-Pluto has a proclivity for seeing hidden agendas, or the stories behind people's lives. This energy is driven to discover hidden passions and situations in one's life and the lives of others. Moon-Pluto can lead to an interest in depth psychology which delves into the unavoidable circumstances into which people are born. This may be seen as a Freudian or Shakespearian energy combination.

MERCURY

Mercury-Venus –
Energy Process: Attraction to the power of a beautiful idea
Behavioral Symptoms: Mercury-Venus gives verbal intelligence and literary ability. There is a knack for words which supports doing well in school. This brings the ability to communicate in a way that is sensitive and interesting; an attractive, even beautiful way. Mercury connects ideas, noticing the appearance and feel of them, how ideas flow & connect, the attraction and movement of one to the next. For Mercury-Venus, thought itself flows beautifully and is full of color and breadth. There is also an appreciation and enjoyment of the verbal and literary skills of others.

Mercury-Mars –
Energy Process: Energizes, stimulates, and acts on mental processes
Behavioral Symptoms: Mercury-Mars needs to learn and understand. This is "the eternal student". This drive inspires a lifetime of learning. They do not trust that everything is OK until they understand it, which leads to a willingness to "fight" to find understanding. It becomes an intense pursuit to understand how things work, along with a passion to act on things learned.

Mercury-Jupiter –
Energy Process: Connects ideas forming an expansive pattern
Behavioral Symptoms: Mercury-Jupiter sees the big picture. It is motivated by big expansive ideas. It cares little for the technical detail, the dotting every "I" and crossing every "T". It is good at integrating and connecting ideas into a larger theme. Mercury-Jupiter looks to big structures, finding interest in history, religion, philosophy, and politics. It wants to understand social trends, social issues, concerns that reach through time and space. It is comfortable in multidisciplinary studies that integrate a myriad of perspectives.

Energy Processes & Behavior Symptoms of Planets/Combinations

Mercury-Saturn –

Energy Process: Analyzing to eliminate the superfluous and find the essence
Behavioral Symptoms: Mercury-Saturn is analysis. The desire is to figure out the technical details, eliminating as many ideas and variables as possible. The goal is to discover and understand the fundamental concept, process, idea, or pattern involved. Mercury-Saturn has the patience needed for tedious work. It often uses a scientific, analytical or academic approach to understanding and learning.

Mercury-Uranus –

Energy Process: Connects ideas in the present moment
Behavioral Symptoms: Mercury-Uranus has a quick, clever, intelligent mind. The attention is here; it is now, in the moment. The "in the moment" focus results in quick mental and physical agility and sharpness. Mercury-Uranus is good at tasks requiring quick reflexes, speed, and agility. Mental focus is sharp and quickly adjusts to external and/or internal stimuli, sometimes bringing a new perspective, suggestion, or insight to a challenge. Long-range planning, attention to detail, or drawn-out problem solving are not easy.

Mercury-Neptune –

Energy Process: Attraction to fascinating, idealistic, visionary thoughts
Behavioral Symptoms: Mercury-Neptune turns on the magic of the mind. It has a fascination with ideas that are often overlooked and that wake up the magic in life. The cognitive process is colored by the magical, fascinating, wonder of life. Thus, it functions well when ideas are presented in fascinating, inspiring ways. Sometimes Mercury-Neptune will not thrive in an education system where the teachers and the environment, stress performance and results. If ideas are presented in too dull and dry a manner, the Mercury-Neptune person will lose interest. They live in an amazing world of wonder and magic and are only attracted to ideas that fit into that world.

Mercury-Pluto –

Energy Process: Connects ideas obsessively or compulsively

Behavioral Symptoms: Mercury-Pluto has strong opinions. It gets fixated on a topic for a long period of time. Through intense mental focus, it can achieve high levels of mastery. This intense driving obsessiveness will push past the limits of everyone else and is often not open or receptive to the ideas of others. A helpful reminder for this energy is to encourage taking a deep breath, stepping back and opening up to the thoughts, interests, and points of view of others, and then continuing with its obsessive-focused way of operating.

VENUS

Venus-Mars –

Energy Process: Accomplishing based on an attraction to the beauty that is alive, visceral, and real

Behavioral Symptoms: Venus-Mars needs to live in a world full of real tangible, sensual life experiences that are tactile and visceral. It uses its energy to create that world. This is the process of attraction with a need to act on that attraction in sensual, tactile, visceral ways. It brings a deeply rooted feeling of being actively alive, awake, and connected to natural elements, such as wood, stone, strong colors, natural fabrics, plants, herbs, etc. Venus-Mars needs to create a life full of the richness of nature. One of the visceral experiences of Venus-Mars in human beings is the attraction of one person to another that is experienced as romantic love. Venus-Mars is repulsed by the digital, virtual, and prefabricated nature of the modern world.

Venus-Jupiter –

Energy Process: Attraction to the beauty that is expansive

Behavioral Symptoms: Venus-Jupiter is outgoing and friendly. It needs to be social, to celebrate life, and not be weighed down by life's responsibilities. It radiates a sense of the expansiveness of life and a feeling of welcoming intimacy where all are welcome. Its primary need is to enjoy life in a big way on a regular basis. It does not want to deal with limiting circumstances or responsibilities. When this basic need is fulfilled, it is better at meeting life's responsibilities.

Energy Processes & Behavior Symptoms of Planets/Combinations

Venus-Saturn –

Energy Process: Attraction to the beauty that gets to the essential core

Behavioral Symptoms: Venus-Saturn has a quintessential elegance: pleasingly simple and neat. It is attracted to sincerity and honesty, with a focus on the important and essential qualities of the person. It puts much more emphasis on the inner character than the outer appearances. There is a desire for maturity and dedication in relationships. A partner needs not to be rich or especially attractive, but rather sincere, real, and honest. It can be an artist because it sees what makes something beautiful. It puts an emphasis on simple lines making elegant designs with a solid foundation. It is able to build a website, remove clutter, or arrange the furniture in a room. Venus-Saturn can easily see what is important and essential, both visually and emotionally.

Venus-Uranus –

Energy Process: Attraction to the beauty that is rhythmic, exciting, and spontaneous

Behavioral Symptoms: Venus-Uranus has sudden attractions. This makes it excitable and improvisational. It needs to express itself rhythmically, dancing or playing music, or attending live concerts to function well. When expressed in its true form the energy is positive and vibrant, if blocked or denied it may manifest as depression. A Venus-Uranus relationship must have an element of spontaneity. Commitment and memory are not enough to hold its interest and it will drift away. It is alive in the moment and even little surprises will enable it to experience life in the moment as being exciting and electrifying.

Venus-Neptune –

Energy Process: An inspired, dreamy attraction to beauty

Behavioral Symptoms: Venus-Neptune needs to experience a romantic feeling that pervades life. All relationships need to be infused with a sense of magic and meaning. Romance is very important, and these individuals crave a dreamy romantic feeling in their relationships. Venus-Neptune needs to experience a sense of magical beauty. It is inspired by the fragrance of flowers or a walk in a special place in the moonlight. It needs to infuse its everyday surroundings and relationships with elements that are magical. Without a sense of magic and romance, Venus-Neptune starts to become apathetic because life loses its meaning.

Venus-Pluto –

Energy Process: Compulsive, obsessive attraction to beauty

Behavioral Symptoms: Venus-Pluto is attracted to some place or person by a passionate, powerful, irresistible, invisible, internal force, an obsession. It must follow a deep, soul-based impulse rising from within. Life choices are based on passion rather than reason. On the surface, its choices may not make sense to others, but that is its passion. If Venus-Pluto is able to follow its soul-level compulsions, its life can become rich, meaningful, and exciting. If not, life can become difficult and there can be mental-emotional issues.

MARS

Mars-Jupiter –

Energy Process: A force of expansive accomplishment

Behavioral Symptoms: Mars-Jupiter wants to achieve big things, and this tends to make it successful. There is a kind of discontent here. By the time it achieves something, it is already focused on the next thing it wants to achieve. It tends to be entrepreneurial, always looking for the next mountain to climb, the next new thing to achieve.

Mars-Saturn –

Energy Process: A force to accomplish the essential things that need to be done

Behavioral Symptoms: Mars-Saturn gets to the basic essentials of the job at hand, bringing precision and efficiency to do the job and doing it well. It can also work on figuring out what the essential essence of something is, cutting through the layers to get to the core. Mars-Saturn finds meaning and gratification in life's challenges. There is an intense drive to work methodically with competency to get a project or goal completed. It is focused on the fundamentals and the details of a project. It will not shy away from a project no matter how dirty, grimy, boring, or non-glamorous it is, it does the dirty work. Mars-Saturn can be taken advantage of because it is more focused on what needs to be done than on how much it is paid.

Energy Processes & Behavior Symptoms of Planets/Combinations

Mars-Uranus –

Energy Process: A sudden burst of energy to achieve a goal

Behavioral Symptoms: Mars-Uranus takes the initiative having an ability to respond quickly. This energy is useful when leadership or innovation is needed and needed now. It brings an explosive burst that gets a project started. It can experience impatience and an impulse to move on to something new. This energy is not interested in doing research and is not good at finishing a project. A side note: if this combination is paired with Mercury-Saturn, they can have the patience to methodically research a project before explosively moving forward with it.

Mars-Neptune –

Energy Process: The force to accomplish one's dream

Behavioral Symptoms: Mars-Neptune needs to express the magic of its dream. Neptune can see the magic in everyday life that most people overlook. This becomes a dream that may not appear to be exotic, spiritual, or unusual. The wonder and magic of the dream, ideal or vision lead to the expression of an infectious or charismatic excitement. This charisma attracts others to aid in achieving the dream. If the pursuit is steadfast, honest, and shared with others, success will most likely result. If frustration sets in and the magic is lost, the unfolding of the dream can be stifled. As one dream is fulfilled or completed, a new one needs to take its place or life will lose meaning.

Mars-Pluto –

Energy Process: A force of obsessive, compulsive achievement

Behavioral Symptoms: Mars-Pluto is driven by passion. This explosive, intense power comes in bursts since it would be impossible to sustain it continuously over a long period of time. Mars-Pluto needs to find a project where it can become fully engaged and immersed. It needs to push the boundaries, force limits, and see how far it can go. A Mars-Pluto lifestyle needs to be able to engage in intensely focused periodic activity/work where it can push hard and engage all its resources.

Jupiter

Jupiter-Saturn –
Energy Process: Essential, regulated growth
Behavioral Symptoms: Jupiter-Saturn is about planning, structures, designs, efficiency, quality control, and all things involving regulated growth. It figures out what is essential and sets up the appropriate goals and structures needed to develop it. Jupiter-Saturn considers the essential to be that which will have value after your life is over. Thus, it creates a solid plan and can bring that plan to fruition. This leads to long-term success and is especially effective in business.

Jupiter-Uranus –
Energy Process: Growth and expansion that is concentrated and electrified by the waves of the moment
Behavioral Symptoms: Jupiter-Uranus is excited, enthusiastic, bubbly, and buoyant. This can lead to "good luck" as it is an energy of exuberance and enthusiasm which can attract helpful people and/or situations. There is a willingness to take risks and to encourage situations or scenarios that foster spontaneity, improvisation, and excitement. Jupiter-Uranus seems to have a positive effect on chance events like winning the lottery, perhaps because of its openness and ability to embrace spontaneous good fortune, thus it is the "good luck" aspect.

Jupiter-Neptune –
Energy Process: Seeking bigger, more expansive fantasies and dreams
Behavioral Symptoms: Jupiter is expansive, and Neptune is idealism, dreams, and visions. Together they will inspire a life moving it beyond the mundane and ordinary into something extraordinary and unusual. It has an attraction to the exotic, the magical, and fantastic places in the physical or non-physical realms. There is a constant desire to move beyond, a sense that there is something better on the other side of the mountain or the other side of the rainbow. Jupiter-Neptune is claustrophobic and dislikes being tied down. It feels it must expand outward.

Jupiter-Pluto –

Energy Process: A compulsive need to become larger and grander

Behavioral Symptoms: Jupiter-Pluto has the capacity to hold a lot of 'power', whether in terms of holding a powerful position in the world or in the realm of 'inner' power. It feels a sense of destiny or mission that is limitless and without constraints. Jupiter-Pluto has an intuitive sense of the depth of meaning that one's life holds, and it is also connected to the deeper levels of meaning within the larger world. This is where this person feels they belong and how this person knows who they are. It is where they are comfortable, and they feel destined to be in surroundings or environments that are grand in scale and quality. They can embrace these grander environments and feel at home in them.

Saturn

Saturn-Uranus –

Energy Process: Uranus modifies and electrifies Saturn's focus making it impatient to get to the essence right now

Behavioral Symptoms: Saturn-Uranus needs clarity and to grasp the essence right now. Saturn-Uranus feels uncomfortable following the rules of others. It needs to develop its own structure rather than using structures designed by others. If constrained by the constant expectation and requirements of others, its free spirit is prone to rebellion. It needs to speak freely, to speak without judgment, and to speak with a sense of truth. This open view is often difficult for other people to deal with. If Saturn-Uranus is forced to deny its free expression, it can become very disturbed resulting in physical symptoms and dysfunctional emotions which can lead to conflict.

Saturn-Neptune –

Energy Process: Removes superficial glitter and glamour to get to honest, sincere, fundamental, long-lasting ideas, ideals, and visions

Behavioral Symptoms: The dreams of Neptune are not necessarily spiritual or extremely idealistic. "Spiritual" requires the "vision" of Neptune in combination with Saturn's discernment of the fundamental concepts that will last past death. Persons with Saturn-Neptune are often spiritual seekers. They desire to separate the essential from the non-essential to uncover the deeper meaning and importance of life. They are searching for something sincere, honest, real, and fundamental to guide their life. They will usually be involved in, or are seeking some sort of religious, spiritual, or esoteric practice or philosophy. They have a distaste for glitter and glamour.

Saturn-Pluto –

Energy Process: Obsessive about removing everything to get to the essence
Behavioral Symptoms: A Saturn-Pluto aspect is severe and can be ascetic. Saturn's desire to get to the essence becomes obsessive and takes everything extraneous out of life. It is interested in ultimate issues like sex, birth, and death, the fundamentals of life. Persons with Saturn-Pluto will sacrifice to reach the goal, the end result. It is that sacrifice and commitment that makes tremendous inner strength possible and allows them to achieve excellence. They can endure hardship for a purpose. One often sees Saturn-Pluto connected to an inner planet in the charts of the world's greatest athletes. These are people who practice compulsively and keep going.

Uranus

Uranus-Neptune –

Energy Process: Amazing, out of this world visionary experiences occurring through attunement to the waves of the moment
Behavioral Symptoms: A Uranus-Neptune aspect is extremely sensitive and wants to have its dreams and visions right now, without waiting for them. It parts the veil to the astral plane, connecting in with the mysteries of the universe. This combination motivates the visionary and is inclined to psychic experiences, depending on the harmonic vibration in which it is operating. Uranus-Neptune needs experiences that make it feel awakened, inspired, and enlightened. It wants its inspirations to lift it off the ground. It needs to feel inspired to be fully alive. The person's visions and dreams can move them far from mundane reality.

This aspect results in a higher sensitivity to drugs. People with this aspect in a three-planet pattern should be aware of the possible negative consequences of indiscriminate use of mind-altering substances or drugs. This aspect is often involved with mental or emotional disturbances.

Energy Processes & Behavior Symptoms of Planets/Combinations

Uranus-Pluto -

Energy Process: Compulsive need to be operating in the moment
Behavioral Symptoms: Uranus-Pluto can be explosive. This combination brings a compulsive need to break free from the constraints of the norm. This is an unstable combination that is unwilling and unable to endure constraints for a long period of time. They need an environment where they can be free without harming themselves or others, such as a musician who is improvising, or a boxer with his/her punching bag. When Uranus-Pluto combines with an inner planet in a three-planet pattern, it creates a combination where the person needs to be themselves and often requires the creation of a different kind of world around them. They may not be able to follow the usual paths in life because of their intense need to always be spontaneous and true to themselves.

Neptune

Neptune-Pluto -

Energy Process: An obsessive need to follow a dream or vision
Behavioral Symptoms: When Neptune-Pluto is connected, the person has a strong sense of mission and purpose. When a vibration has a strong Neptune-Pluto aspect, the sense of mission and purpose becomes a dominant characteristic. When Neptune and Pluto combine with an inner planet in a tight pattern in the natal chart, this person has a deep sense of meaning or destiny for being alive. The dream is not necessarily inflexible, but it gives a sense of divine destiny that they will pursue. This sense of mission and purpose unfolds, and they need to follow it in their own way. If pressured to pursue someone else's path they experience deep frustration. They can become apathetic, miserable, or depressed. When Neptune is involved with Pluto, the dream or vision becomes the mission and purpose in one's life.

Vibrational Astrology Study Guide Module One

C. Summary: Energy Processes of Planets/Combinations

Note: The parentheses in red indicate a "catch phrase", a distinctive trait or characteristic present.

Planets

Sun – (Clear & present reality)
The Sun connects us to the current moment and regulates what we are conscious of at any given time.

Moon – (Past into the present)
The Moon brings the past into the present regulating what elements of the past we are aware of.

Mercury – (Makes mental connections)
Mercury makes mental connections and communicates; sees relationships and associations, noticing and comparing similarities and differences.

Venus – (Attraction to beauty)
Venus regulates the magnetic power of attraction to beauty.

Mars - (A force to achieve, drive)
Mars is the dynamic force needed to achieve, the drive to reach a goal.

Jupiter – (Grows & expands)
Jupiter is the energy force that grows and expands. Without Jupiter, there is no growth.

Saturn – (Removes all that is superficial)
Saturn is the energy force that removes all that is superficial to discover the essence, the foundations, the essential core.

Uranus – (Acts spontaneously)
Uranus is the energy force that acts in the current moment without regard for the past or future.

Neptune – (Attraction to dreams, visions, ideals)
Neptune is the force of attraction to dreams, visions, ideals.

Pluto - (Compulsive & obsessive energy)
Pluto is energy from the deep past that expresses itself forcefully as compulsiveness or even obsession.

Energy Processes & Behavior Symptoms of Planets/Combinations

Planet Combinations
Sun

Sun-Moon – *(Brings past into present view)*
Appreciates how the past is the basis or foundation of the present bringing the hidden or shadowed into the light of the present

Sun-Mer – *(Speaks, writes clearly)*
Brings clear and present thought and communication

Sun-Ven – *(Appreciation of simplistic beauty)*
A clear and present beauty

Sun-Mars – *(Loves activity in work & play)*
A clear and present force to achieve, a drive to do something tangible, something real

Sun-Jup – *(Desires growth)*
A clear and present ongoing growth and expansion

Sun-Sat – *(Focus on essentials)*
A clear and present desire to get rid of everything that is not essential

Sun-Ura – *(Spontaneous, quick to laugh & respond)*
Attunes to the waves and cycles of the moment expressing them as a clear and present spontaneity

Sun-Nep – *(Child-like optimism)*
Brings a clear and present sense of attraction to the wonder and magic of dreams, visions, and ideals

Sun-Plu – *(Life of passion & mission)*
Makes daily life compulsive and obsessive.

Moon

Moon-Mer – *(Thoughts of past)*
Thinking about the past and how the past influences the present

Moon-Ven – *(Attracted to soul, depth, long heritage)*
Attraction to the beauty of the past

Moon-Mars – *(Wants to achieve, accomplish)*
Enjoys the feeling of accomplishment and is always seeking to improve its skills

Moon-Jup – *(Warm, friendly, welcoming)*
Has expansive moods and enjoys an open atmosphere

Moon-Sat – *(Sincere, quiet, introverted)*
Has a need for isolation that quiets the emotions enabling one to perceive deep essential long-lasting truths
Moon-Ura – *(Emotionally Impulsive)*
Needs to feel free and unrestricted by expectations and consequences
Moon-Nep – *(Emotionally sensitive)*
Sensitive to the atmosphere and mood
Moon-Plu – *(Compulsive eruptions of feeling)*
Powerful concentrations of past feelings erupt forcefully into the present

Mercury

Mer-Ven – *(Verbal intelligence, Literary ability)*
Attraction to the power of a beautiful idea
Mer-Mar – *(Needs to learn & understand)*
Energizes, stimulates, and acts on mental processes
Mer-Jup – *(Open-minded; Sees big picture)*
Connects ideas together forming an expansive pattern
Mer-Sat – *(Analytical)*
Analyzing to eliminate the superfluous and find the essence
Mer-Ura – *(Clever, Quick thinker)*
Connects ideas in the present moment
Mer-Nep – *(See magic and wonder in life)*
Attraction to fascinating, idealistic, visionary thoughts
Mer-Plu – *(Opinionated)*
Connects ideas obsessively or compulsively

Energy Processes & Behavior Symptoms of Planets/Combinations

Venus

Ven-Mars – *(Needs tangible, sensual life experiences)*
Accomplishing based on an attraction to the beauty that is alive, visceral, and real

Ven-Jup – *(Outgoing & Friendly)*
Attraction to the beauty that is expansive

Ven-Sat – *(Sincere & Honest)*
Attraction to the beauty that gets to the essential core

Ven-Ura – *(Rhythm, Dance, Music)*
Attraction to the beauty that is rhythmic, exciting, and spontaneous

Ven-Nep – *(Magic & Romance)*
An inspired, dreamy attraction to beauty

Ven-Plu – *(Passionate, powerful, irresistible internal force)*
Compulsive, obsessive attraction to beauty

Mars

Mars-Jup – *(Wants to achieve big things)*
A force of expansive accomplishment

Mars-Sat – *(Does the "dirty work")*
A force to accomplish the essential things that need to be done

Mars-Ura – *(Ability to respond quickly)*
A sudden burst of energy to achieve a goal

Mar-Nep – *(Sees magic in everyday life)*
The force to accomplish one's dream

Mar-Plu - *(Driven by passion)*
A force of obsessive, compulsive achievement

Jupiter

Jup-Sat – *(Planning & strategy)*
Essential, regulated growth

Jup-Ura – *(Excited, enthusiastic, "Good Luck" Aspect)*
Growth and expansion that is concentrated and electrified by the waves of the moment

Jup-Nep – *(Gives Inspiration)*
Seeking bigger, more expansive fantasies and dreams

Jup-Plu – *(Has a sense of destiny & mission)*
A compulsive need to become larger and grander

Saturn

Sat-Ura – *(Brings clarity now)*
Uranus modifies and electrifies Saturn's focus making it impatient to get to the essence right now

Sat-Nep – *(Uncovers deeper meaning of life)*
Removes superficial glitter and glamour to get to honest, sincere, fundamental, long-lasting ideas, ideals, and visions

Sat-Plu – *(Severe, Ascetic)*
Obsessive about removing everything to get to the essence

Uranus

Ura-Nep – *(Sensitive, May be visionary)*
Amazing, out of this world visionary experiences occurring through attunement to the waves of the moment

Ura-Plu – *(Needs freedom)*
A compulsive need to be operating in the moment

Neptune

Nep-Plu – *(Mission & purpose)*
An obsessive need to follow a dream or vision

Energy Processes & Behavior Symptoms of Planets/Combinations

D. Books & Videos

Books
Berry, Linda & Cochrane, David, *Vibrational Astrology, Interpreting Aspects*, Gainesville: Cosmic Patterns Software, inc., 2016 (Order through http://www.Lulu.com)

Cochrane, David, *Vibrational Astrology, the Essentials,* Gainesville, Florida: Cosmic Patterns Software, Inc, 2021

Videos
Astrology Tutorial Videos by David Cochrane
Https://www.astrologydc.com

Introduction to VA Course, Part 1
Interpreting Planets: The Energetic Process Behind the Archetypes
Meaning of Sun, Moon, and Planets in Vibrational Astrology
Saturn is Not Malefic: Understanding the Planet Saturn
Sirius Astrology Software: Introduction to Harmonic Astrology

Notes

Notes

Vibrational Astrology Study Guide Module One

CHAPTER 3: Aspects & Orbs

    A. Aspect Glyphs
    B. Ptolemaic Aspects
    C. Non-Ptolemaic Aspects
    D. VA Aspect Interpretation
    E. Proportional Orbs in Vibrational Charts
    F. Aspect Rules for Vibrational Charts
    G. Active and Inactive Aspect Circuits
    H. Aspect Patterns in VA
    I. Aspect Grids
    J. Summary: Aspects & Orbs
    K. Books & Videos

Prime components in Vibrational Astrology are planetary aspects. Aspects are the angular distance, measured in degrees of arc, between two planets within a 360° astrology chart. Aspects determine the interaction between two or more planets. When connected in combinations of three or more following specific rules, the planets with the aspects create a specific energy flow within a person that is expressed as an internal or external behavior. The orb of exactitude of an aspect determines the strength of the energy flow and is one of the factors indicating the importance of a particular vibration.

Note: Detailed instructions related to chart settings apply to users of Sirius 3.0 Astrology Software.

A. Aspect Glyphs

The aspect glyphs on the **Natal Chart** help identify the aspect. Ptolemaic aspects may also be identified using the sign Elements, Modes, or separation of Signs. Non-Ptolemaic aspects may be identified using line color, a solid or dashed aspect line, degrees of separation, and/or the glyphs in the Aspect Grid. The latter techniques become important since the aspect lines in **Vibrational Charts** only have the natal aspect fraction on the aspect line.

Figure 1: Aspect Glyphs

0°	Conjunction	☌	Semisquare	∠	45°
180°	Opposition	☍	Sesquiquadrate	⚼	135°
90°	Square	□	Semisextile	⚺	30°
120°	Trine	△	Quincunx	⚻	150°
60°	Sextile	✶			

Copyright © The Avalon School of Astrology, Inc. All Rights Reserved
All chart wheels and reports used in this module are created from Sirius 3.0 with permission from Cosmic Patterns Software

Aspects & Orbs

B. Ptolemaic Aspects

The five Ptolemaic aspects are **Conjunction (0°), Opposition (180°)(1/2), Square (90°)(1/4), Trine (120°)(1/3), and Sextile (60°)(1/6)**. The first parenthesis shows the degrees of the aspect; the second parenthesis shows the fractional representation of that aspect in the 360° zodiac.

Conjunctions and Oppositions are easily recognized in the chart. In **Figure 2**, Moon-Mars-Uranus, Sun-Mercury, and Venus-Jupiter are **Conjunction** aspects. These planets lie adjacent to one another within a 16° orb. The 16° orb for conjunctions sets the basis for proportional orbs. The orbs must be proportional for the aspects to parallel the aspects in the vibrational charts. The concept of Proportional Orbs is discussed in greater detail in Chapter 3 Section E.

Also, in **Figure 2**, the conjunction of Sun-Mercury is in **Opposition** to Pluto. Planets in Opposition are separated by approximately 180° with up to an 8° orb. In this case, Mercury opposes Pluto with an orb of 2°24' and the Sun opposes Pluto with an orb of 7°53'.

Figure 2: Conjunction, Opposition, & Trine

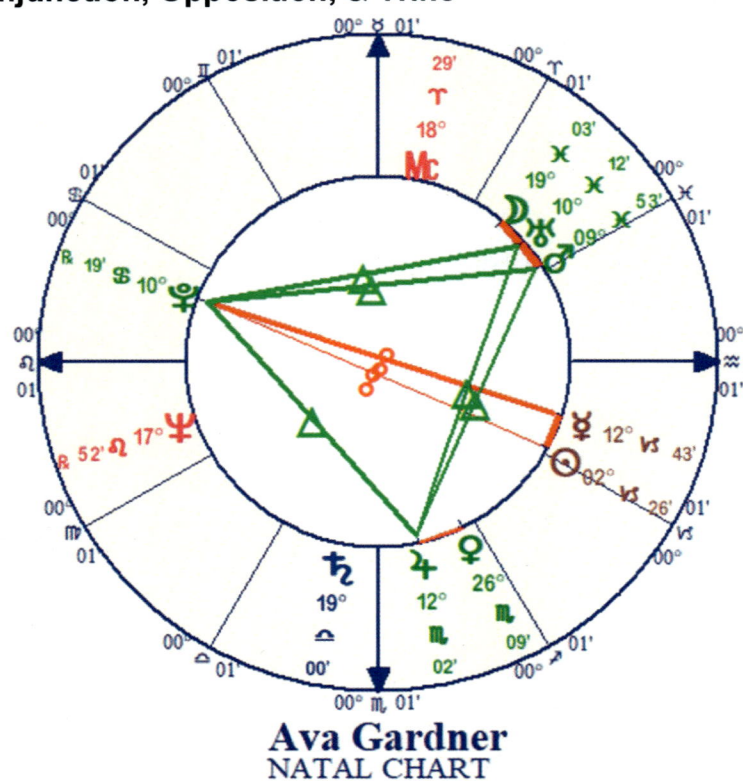

Ava Gardner
NATAL CHART

Vibrational Astrology Study Guide Module One

Trines, Squares, and **Sextiles** are easily identified utilizing the Elements, Modes, and Signs. Signs will be discussed in greater detail in Module 2, Chapter 8.

Planets that **Trine** each other are in 120° aspect (Orb: 5°20') in signs of the same **Element (Fire, Earth, Air or Water).** (4 Signs apart)

SIGN ELEMENTS		SIGNS		
FIRE	Aries ♈	Leo ♌	Sagittarius ♐
EARTH	Taurus ♉	Virgo ♍	Capricorn ♑
AIR	Gemini ♊	Libra ♎	Aquarius ♒
WATER	Cancer ♋	Scorpio ♏	Pisces ♓

In **Figure 2**, the conjunction of Mars-Uranus is **Trine** Pluto. The Mars-Uranus conjunction is in Pisces and Pluto is in Cancer. Pisces and Cancer are four signs apart and Water signs. Mars-Uranus is also **Trine** Jupiter. Jupiter is in Scorpio, another Water sign.

Planets that **Square** each other are in **90° aspect** (Orb: 4°00') in signs of the same **Mode (Cardinal, Fixed, or Mutable).** (3 signs apart)

SIGN MODES		SIGNS			
CARDINAL	Aries ♈	Cancer ♋	Libra ♎	Capricorn ♑
FIXED	Taurus ♉	Leo ♌	Scorpio ♏	Aquarius ♒
MUTABLE	Gemini ♊	Virgo ♍	Sagittarius ♐	Pisces ♓

In **Figure 3**, the Moon-Saturn and Saturn-Neptune are in **Square** aspect. The Moon is in Aquarius (Fixed sign), Saturn is in Scorpio (Fixed sign) and Neptune is in Leo (Fixed sign) (Three signs apart).

When planets are **two signs apart (60°)**(Orb: 2°40'), they are **Sextile** to each other.

In **Figure 3**, Venus is **Sextile** Jupiter. Venus is at 28°45' Aries and Jupiter is at 26°50' Aquarius. Aries and Aquarius are two signs apart, therefore the planets are **Sextile** one another.

Aspects & Orbs

Figure 3: Square & Sextile

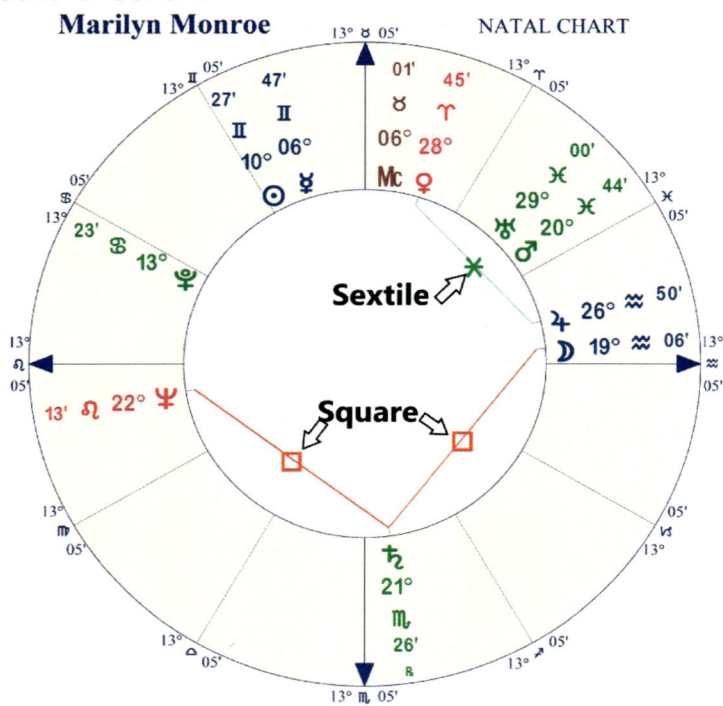

Figure 4: Signs: Elements (matching colors) & Modes

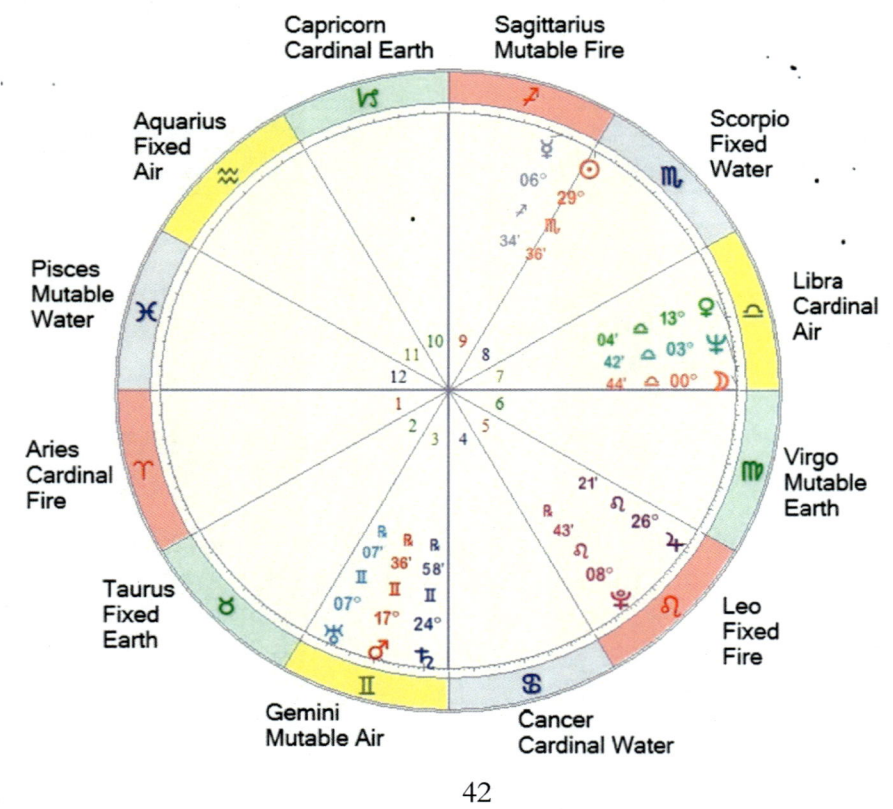

42
Copyright © The Avalon School of Astrology, Inc. All Rights Reserved
All chart wheels and reports used in this module are created from Sirius 3.0 with permission from Cosmic Patterns Software.

Vibrational Astrology Study Guide Module One

The Ptolemaic aspects in the Natal Chart may be identified by their respective glyph on the aspect line **(Figure 5)** or in the Vibrational Charts, by the criteria above, line color, degrees of separation, and/or the glyph in the aspect grid. **(Figure 6)**

Figure 5: Ptolemaic Aspects in Natal Chart

Figure 6: Ptolemaic Aspects in a Vibrational Chart

43

Copyright © The Avalon School of Astrology, Inc. All Rights Reserved
All chart wheels and reports used in this module are created from Sirius 3.0 with permission from Cosmic Patterns Software

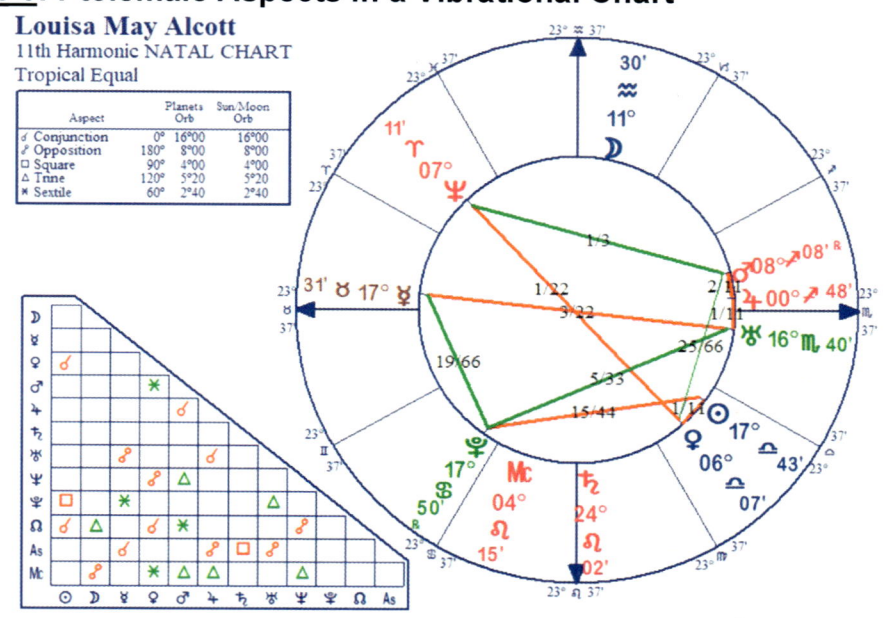

Aspects & Orbs

In the Vibrational Chart **(Figure 6)**, the fractions on the aspect lines show the aspects in the Natal Chart.

C. Non-Ptolemaic Aspects

The Non-Ptolemaic aspects are **Semisquare (45°)(⅛), Sesquiquadrate (135°)(⅜), Semisextile (30°)(1/12), Quincunx (150°)(5/12) and 1/16th aspect (22.5°)(1/16)**. The first parenthesis shows the degrees of the aspect; the second shows the fractional representation of that aspect in the 360° chart.

The Non-Ptolemaic aspects are identified by the aspect glyph or a dashed line in the Natal Chart. **(Figures 7&8)** In the Vibrational Chart, the aspects may be identified by line color, a solid or dashed aspect line, degrees of separation, and/or glyph in the Aspect Grid. **(Figure 9)**

<u>Figure 7</u>: Non-Ptolemaic Aspects: Semisquare, Sesquiquadrate, Semisextile, Quincunx (Natal Chart)

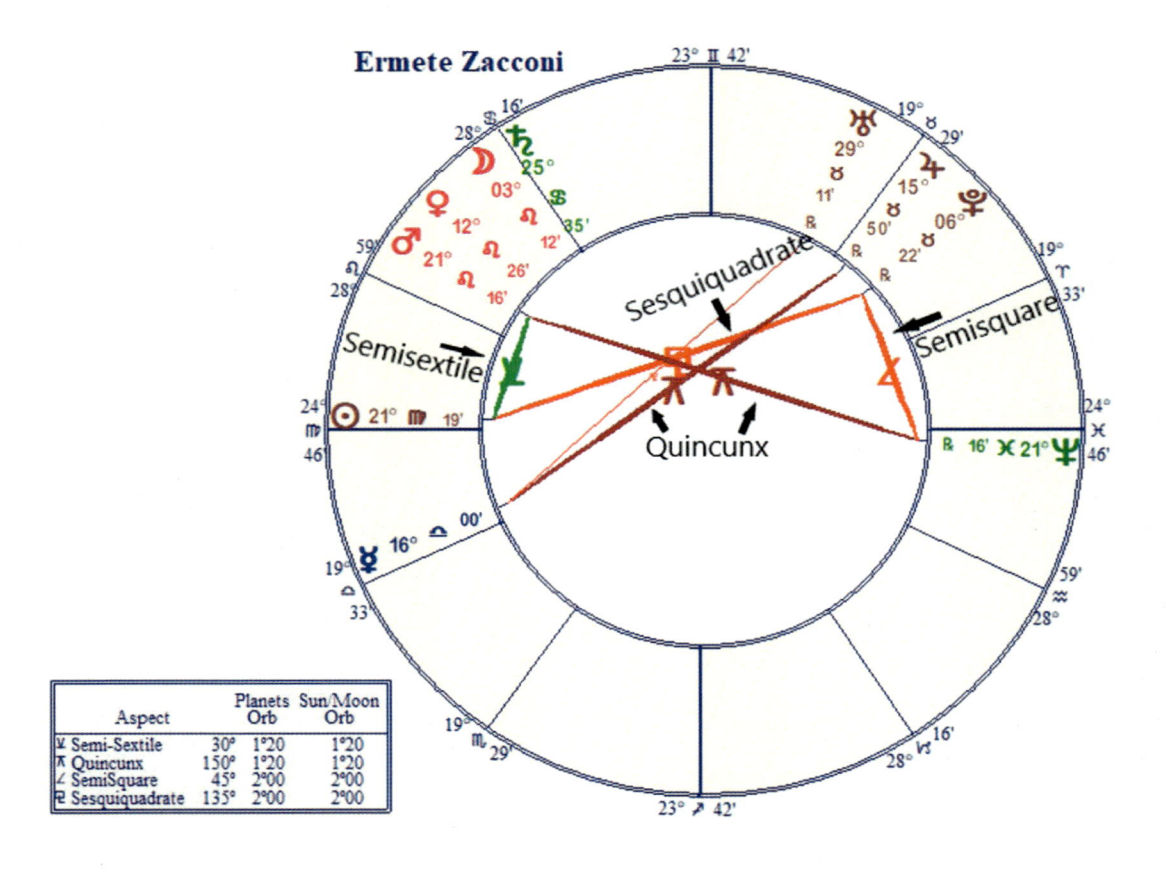

Copyright © The Avalon School of Astrology, Inc. All Rights Reserved
All chart wheels and reports used in this module are created from Sirius 3.0 with permission from Cosmic Patterns Software.

Vibrational Astrology Study Guide Module One

Figure 8: **1/16th aspects (22.5° or 1/16)** are read by a dashed red line in both Natal and Vibrational charts.

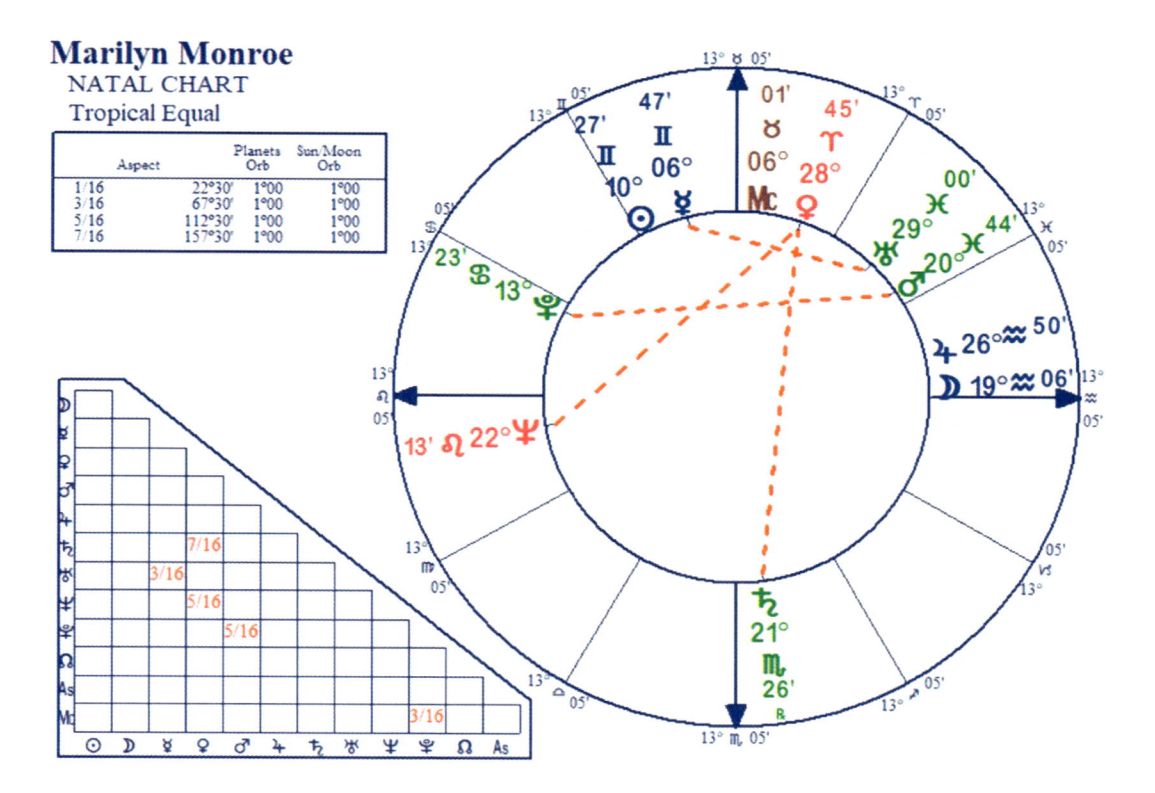

Aspects & Orbs

Figure 9: Non-Ptolemaic Aspects in 19-Vibration Chart

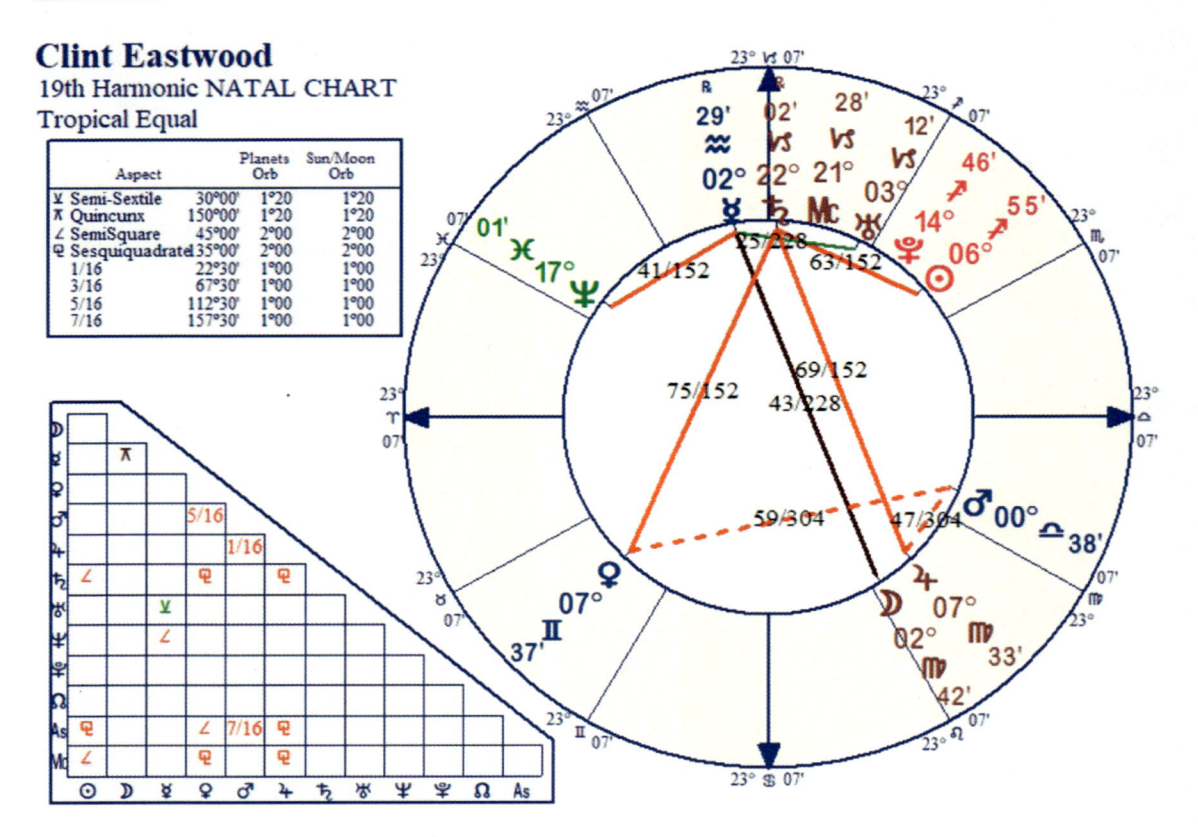

Semi-Sextile: Mercury - Uranus
Quincunx: Moon - Mercury
SemiSquare: Sun - Saturn; Mercury - Neptune
Sesquiquadrate: Venus - Saturn; Jupiter - Saturn
1/16th: Mars - Jupiter
5/16th: Venus - Mars

46
Copyright © The Avalon School of Astrology, Inc. All Rights Reserved
All chart wheels and reports used in this module are created from Sirius 3.0 with permission from Cosmic Patterns Software.

Vibrational Astrology Study Guide Module One

D. VA Aspect Interpretation

In interpretation, three things must be combined: The Vibration, The Planetary Energy, and The Aspect.

The vibration gives the basic rules under which the planets and their aspects must operate. Each planetary aspect adds additional information about how that pair of planets functions. Each aspect is interpreted in combination with the meaning of the vibration and the meanings of the planets in the vibration.

The meanings of the aspects are:

Conjunction (0°) - Conjunctions involve planets that are adjacent to one another and get their meaning from the planets that aspect them. Combine their meanings with the vibration they occupy. They show the basic energy expressions and driving force in a person's life.

Opposition (180°) (½) - Oppositions create a polarity between the planets. The focus is on sharing or conflicting with others.

Square (90°) (1/4) – Squares are a need to take action, providing the motivation and drive to do something, make changes, make progress or achieve a goal in response to a drive within.

Trine (120°) (1/3) - Trines show an unrestricted energy flow that is easy and tends to be smooth.

Sextile (60°) (1/6) - Sextiles want to share in an easy, free-flowing manner. With this aspect, a person is inclined to have pleasant conversations and interactions with others.

Semisquare (45°) (1/8) - Semisquares are what one has to do. They define one's mode of operation when one takes action.

Sesquiquadrate (135°) (3/8) - Sesquiquadrates are similar to Semisquares except that they are more easily and naturally expressed and somewhat less stressful.

Semisextile (30°) (1/12) - Semisextiles balance action and flow. They are a strongly ingrained quality.

Aspects & Orbs

Quincunx (150°) (5/12) – Quincunxes represent energies that need to be developed. The vibration is the main descriptor of the growth needed with the two planets further refining the growth process. There is a strong motivation for these energies to develop into a useful mature behavior. If this growth process is unsuccessful, this trait will not be available in this vibration.

1/16, 3/16, 5/16, 7/16th aspects (22.5°) (1/16) - The 1/16th aspects indicate an action that originates in conscious internal processing that is not obvious to others.

Aspect fractions with the same denominator (or multiples of the same denominator) will have a similar meaning. The denominator of the aspect fraction in the natal chart designates the vibration in which that aspect will be a conjunction. The numerator brings small modifications to the vibration meaning, which are generally not used in readings.

E. Proportional Orbs in Vibrational Charts

An orb is the allowable difference between the primary arc and the exact aspect. An aspect's strength is determined by the exactitude of the orb. The smaller the orb the stronger the aspect, the larger the orb the weaker the aspect. The orbs used in VA may appear large, i.e., conjunction = 16°. Utilizing a proportional comparison to the other aspects, the value may not be as large as it seems.

A complete list of the allowable and "strong" aspect orbs for VA Charts is shown in **Figure 10**. The "Calculation" column shows how the orb was calculated. The conjunction orb (16°) is divided by the denominator of the aspect fraction. These are called proportional orbs. *The orbs must be proportional for the aspects to parallel the natal aspects in the vibrational charts.* The "Strong Orb" category is approximately 1/3rd of the maximum allowable orb. (**Figure 10**)

<u>Figure 10</u>: **VA Aspect Proportional Orbs**

Aspect	Max Orb	Strong Orb	Fraction	Calculation
Ptolemaic Aspects				
Conjunction (0°)	16°	5°20'	1	(16/1)
Opposition (180°)	8°	2°40'	1/2	(16/2)
Square (90°)	4°	1°20'	1/4	(16/4)
Trine (120°)	5°20'	1°45'	1/3	(16/3)
Sextile (60°)	2°40'	0°50'	1/6	(16/6)
Non-Ptolemaic Aspects				
SemiSquare (45°)	2°00'	0°40'	1/8	(16/8)
Sesquiquadrate (135°)	2°00	0°40'	3/8	(16/8)
Semi-Sextile (30°)	1°20'	0°25'	1/12	(16/12)
Quincunx (150°)	1°20'	0°25'	5/12	(16/12)
1/16th Aspect (22.5°)	1°00	0°20'	1/16	(16/16)

Aspects & Orbs

F. Aspect Rules for Vibrational Charts

Listed below are the color settings for aspect lines used in Vibrational Astrology.
Solid Red: Conjunction, Opposition, Square, Semisquare, Sesquiquadrate
Dashed Red Lines: 1/16th aspect
Solid Green Lines: Trine, Sextile and Semisextile
Solid Brown Lines: Quincunx

To add fractions to the vibrational aspect lines (Sirius Astrology Software):
1. Right-click in the white space containing the chart, a window titled "Wheel Style" will appear.
2. Click "Customize" at the bottom of the "Wheel Style" window.
3. Another window "Customize Wheel" appears. Click "Aspects" in the tabs at the top of this inset.
4. An Aspect Listing inset will appear. Normally, the category of aspects titled "Harmonic, Med. Major Only" needs to be marked. Then Click "Customize this Aspect Set" at the bottom of the list, Click "OK"
5. The "Change Aspect" Screen appears. At the bottom of this screen, left of center, check the box for "Natal Aspect Shown on Aspect Line in Harmonic Chart".

Note: Aspect colors and lines may also be set on this screen. Be sure "Varies by Orb" is checked in the Line Characteristics.

6. Click "OK", "OK", "OK" to return to the chart screen

Apply the following rules to identify aspect circuits in vibrational charts. In all cases, you must have at least 3 planets connected to each other, to form a 3-planet energy pattern:
a. All planets (3 or more) connected by "Solid Red" aspect lines may be read.
b. All planets (3 or more) connected by "Solid Green" aspect lines may be read.
c. Combining Red and Green aspects: "Red" conjunction or opposition aspects combine with "Green" aspects when in a pattern of 3 or more planets.

The **Quincunx** and **1/16th aspects** are regarded as special situations.

The **Quincunx** is NOT included in energy circuits but is dealt with separately in the natal and vibrational charts. The energy may be interpreted as a potential trait in the chart in which it appears. The **Quincunx** (5/12) describes a point of growth for traits or characteristics. There is a sense of something lacking which provides a motivation to change. The two planets involved need to learn to work together in that vibration.

Vibrational Astrology Study Guide Module One

The **1/16, 3/16, 5/16, and 7/16ths aspects** form energy circuits. The **1/16th aspects** indicate conscious internal processing where one acts based on the results of that processing. When **1/16th aspects** are significantly present in a circuit, the planets are more easily interpreted when one doubles (2X) the vibration. **(Figure 11)**

Figure 11: 5-Vibration 1/16th Aspects in the 10-Vibration Chart

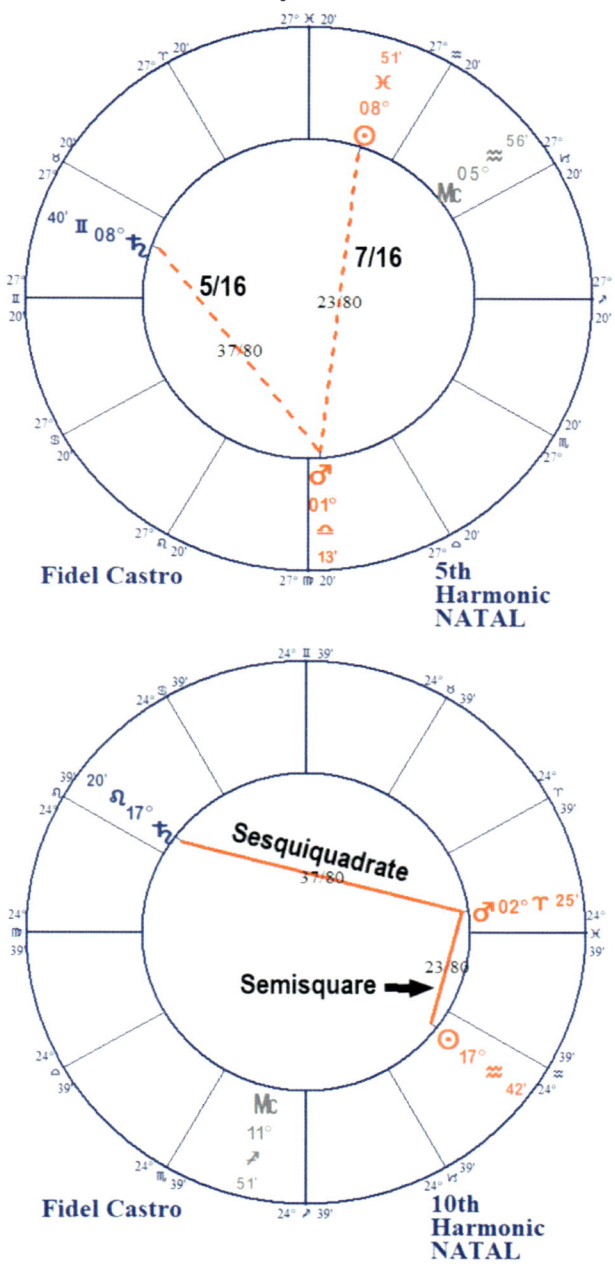

Fidel Castro — 5th Harmonic NATAL

Fidel Castro — 10th Harmonic NATAL

Aspects & Orbs

In **Figure 11**, the **5/16th aspect** has become a **Sesquiquadrate** (3/8th aspect) and the **7/16th aspect** has become a **Semisquare** (1/8th aspect). The **Sesquiquadrate** and **Semisquare** may be used to complete energy circuits of three or more planets.

There are no unaspected planets in VA. In VA, planet combinations are viewed as energy processes. Two planet combinations in the natal chart would be felt as an internal trait and not necessarily a behavior pattern. Three or more planets are required for the energy to flow as a behavior pattern.

G: Active and Inactive Aspect Circuits

All aspect circuits of three planets or more in a vibration must have at least one fraction denominator on one of the aspect lines that is evenly divisible by the vibration to be active in that circuit. Only one aspect line that is evenly divisible is sufficient to connect the aspect circuit into the vibration. **(Figure 12)**

Figure 12: Active Aspect Circuit - Circuit Connected to 8-Vibration (Denominator 24/8=3 (evenly divisible))

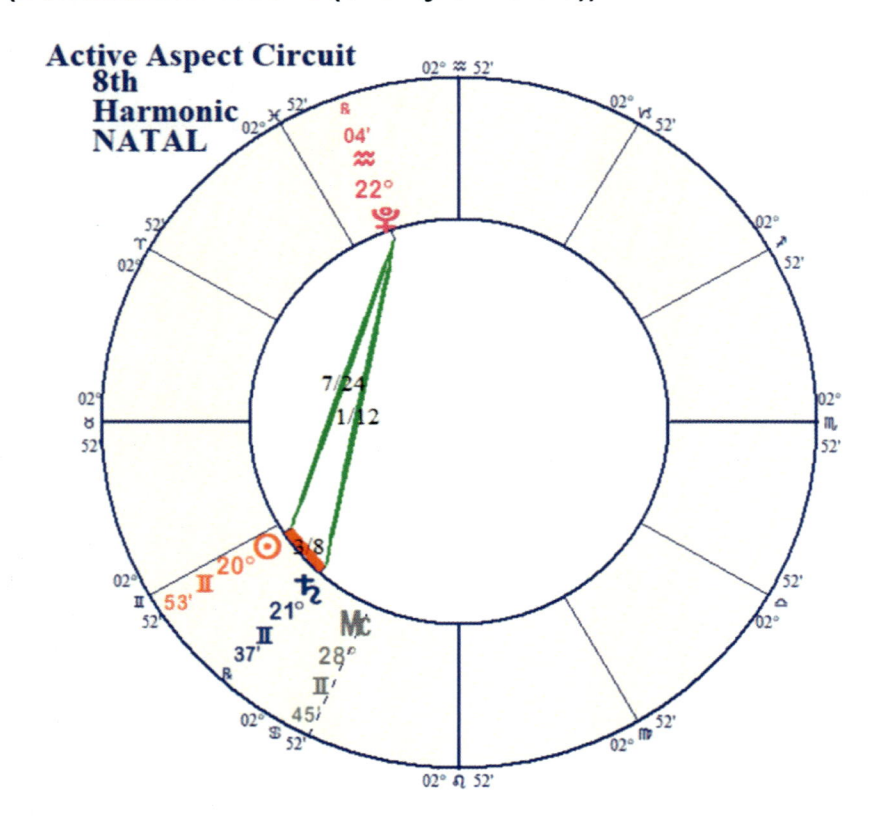

If no aspect fractions connect the circuit into the vibration, that circuit is not active in that vibration and **cannot** be read in that vibration. (**Figure 13**)

Figure 13: Inactive Aspect Circuit - Circuit NOT Connected to 9-Vibration
(Denominators 8,12,24 are **not** evenly divisible by 9)

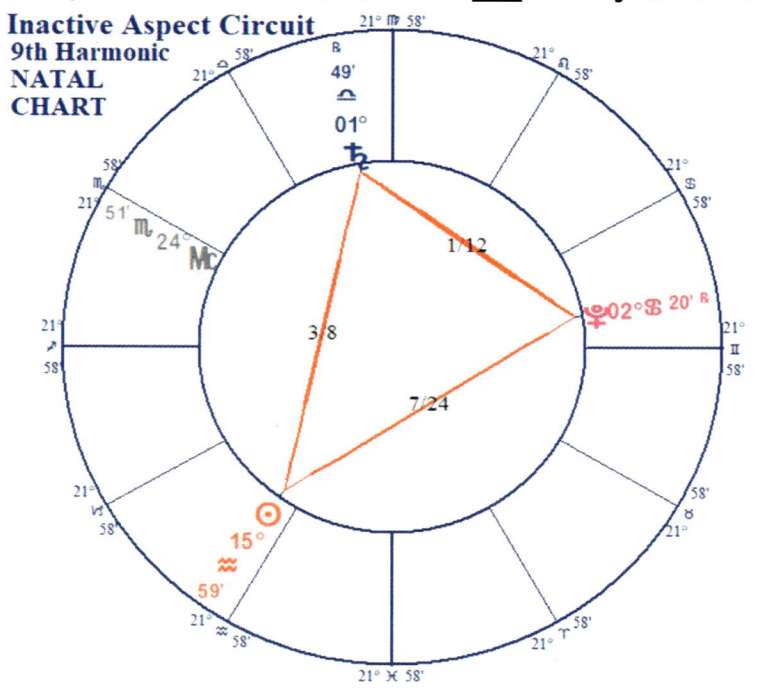

Figures 12 & 13 are from the chart of the same individual and reflect the same three planets in each vibrational chart. The aspects can be read in the 8-Vibration since the denominator (24) is evenly divisible by the vibration (8). (**Figure 12**) In the 9-Vibration, none of the denominators (8, 12, or 24) are evenly divisible by the vibration (9). Therefore, the circuit cannot be read in the 9-Vibration. (**Figure13**).

The goal of Vibrational Astrology is to help identify planetary energy patterns in a person's life, some of which the person may be unaware of. Increasing awareness can support self-development. **The chart shows how the energy wants or needs to flow, not how it will manifest.** A tight aspect pattern that is active in the vibration indicates a strong need in the person. The goal is to understand how the energy wants to flow and to figure out how that pattern can be expressed in a way that is compatible with the person's life and character.

Aspects & Orbs

Planets are understood to each have a simple basic energy. These energies are combined or linked by the planetary aspects. Aspects containing the Inner Planets (Sun, Moon, Mercury, Venus, Mars) generate behaviors that one identifies with, feeling as if that person is the source of those thought processes, feelings, attractions, motivations, etc.

An aspect circuit consisting solely of planets beyond Mars (Jupiter, Saturn, Uranus, Neptune, Pluto) results in an experience that feels like it is coming from outside. These impersonal aspect patterns can still be strong determiners of behavior. If there are one or more inner planets involved with the outer planets, the behavior will be experienced as personal.

H. Aspect Patterns in VA

There are numerous names for various multi-planet aspect patterns in all areas of astrology. In VA, only five aspect patterns are identified by name: **Grand Trine, T-Square, Yod, Grand Cross,** and the **Kite**. A pattern name provides an easy way to reflect the increased planetary energies in an aspect pattern. All other patterns are described by the aspects composing the circuit.

Figure 14: Grand Trine: Three planets connected by Trine aspects (approximately 120° apart, within orb) in the same Element (Fire, Earth, Air, Water)

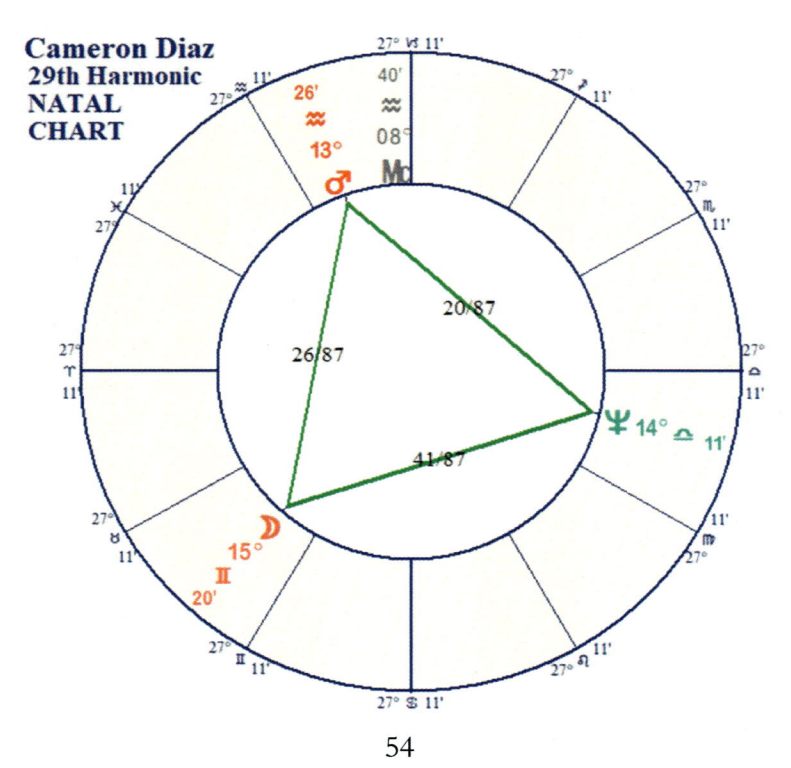

Copyright © The Avalon School of Astrology, Inc. All Rights Reserved
All chart wheels and reports used in this module are created from Sirius 3.0 with permission from Cosmic Patterns Software.

Vibrational Astrology Study Guide Module One

Figure 15: T-Square: Three planets, two defined by an Opposition aspect with the third Squaring the two oppositional planets

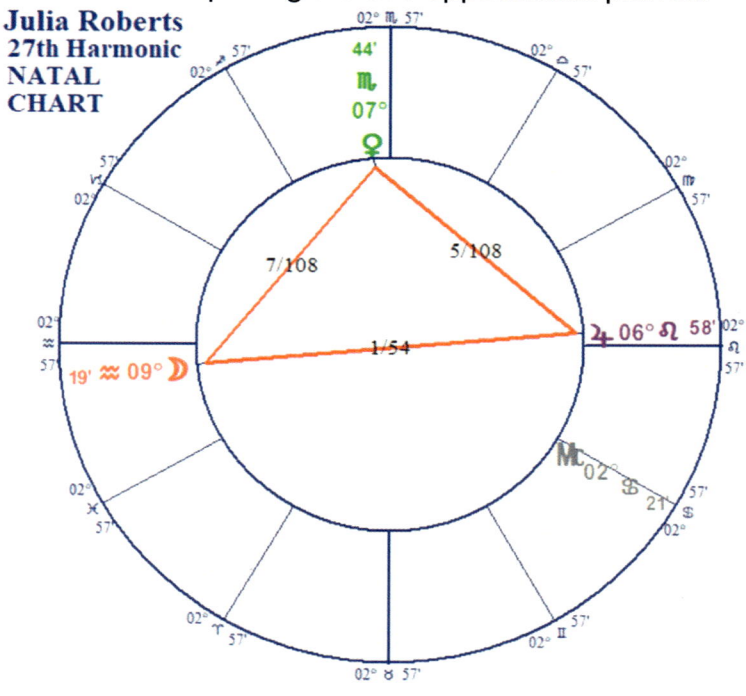

Figure 16: Yod: Three planets connected by two Quincunxes and a Sextile

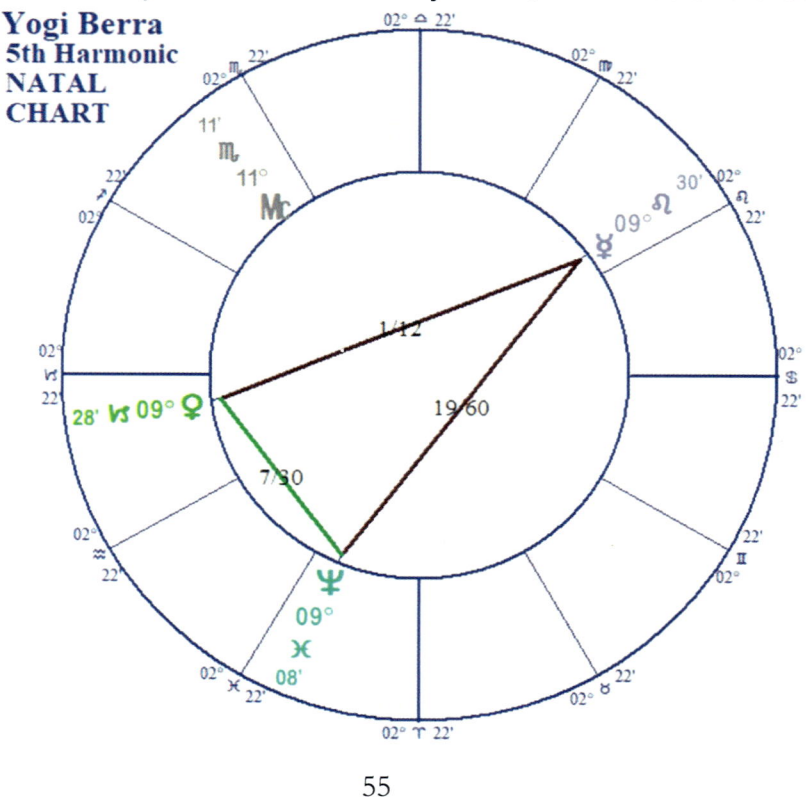

55
Copyright © The Avalon School of Astrology, Inc. All Rights Reserved
All chart wheels and reports used in this module are created from Sirius 3.0 with permission from Cosmic Patterns Software

Aspects & Orbs

Figure 17: Grand Cross: Four planets all located approximately Square (90° apart within orb), the Opposition planets creating a cross

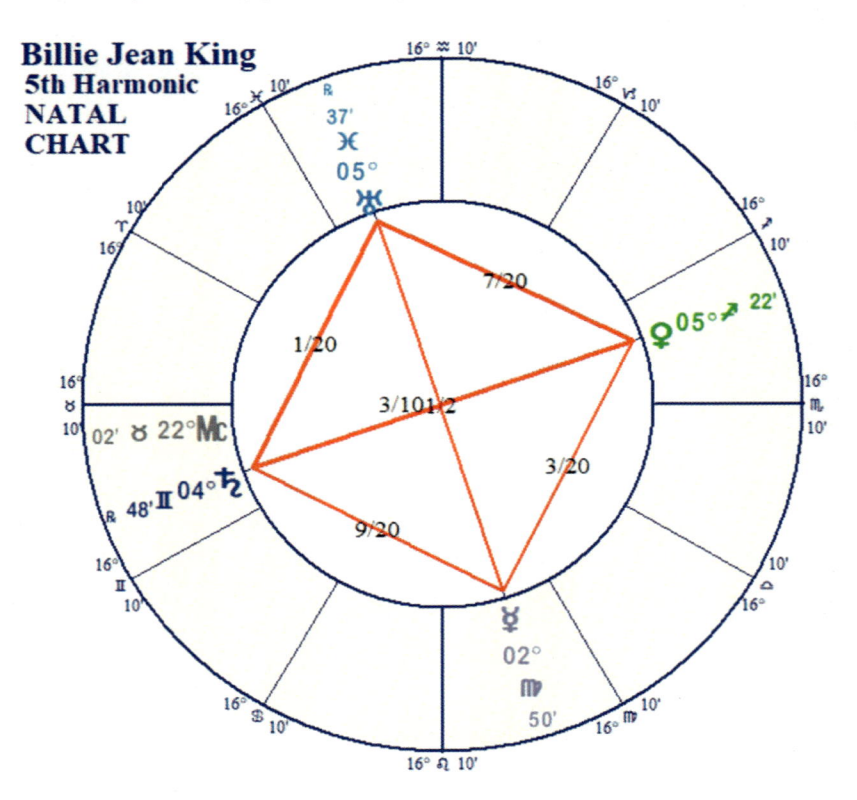

56
Copyright © The Avalon School of Astrology, Inc. All Rights Reserved
All chart wheels and reports used in this module are created from Sirius 3.0 with permission from Cosmic Patterns Software.

"Power" aspect structure: It is not uncommon for a planetary conjunction to be part of a larger planetary structure. The word, "Power", preceding an aspect structure (or midpoint structure) describes a conjunction that adds an additional planet to the structure, thereby increasing the structure's significance in the life of the person.

Figure 18: Kite (Power Kite): Four planet aspect pattern composed of a Grand Trine with one planet Opposite one of the points of the Grand Trine (all within orb) (Looks like a Kite!) The Conjunction of Moon-Saturn creates a **Power Kite**.

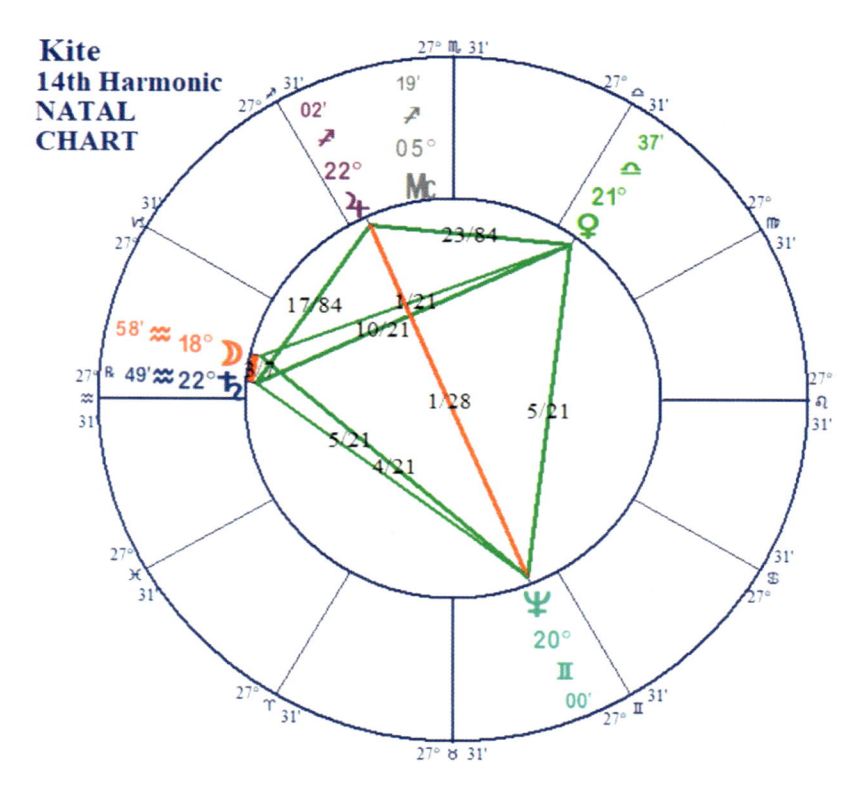

Aspects & Orbs

Figure 19: Power Grand Trine: The Conjunction of Sun-Jupiter adds extra energy to the Grand Trine structure.

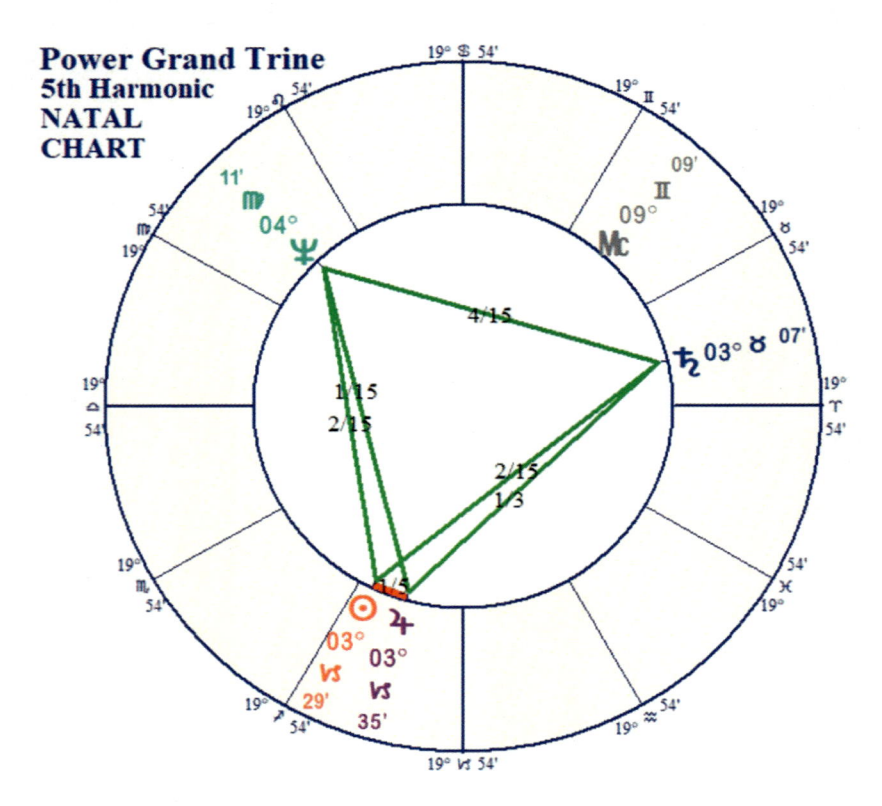

Any aspect structure where two sets of Conjunctions add planets to the configuration in different single planetary positions would have the prefix, "Double Power". Two sets of planetary conjunctions on separate corners of a Grand Trine would be called a **Double Power Grand Trine. (Figure 20)**

Figure 20: **Double Power Grand Trine:** The Conjunctions of Venus-Mars and Neptune-Pluto increase the energy in this Grand Trine structure.

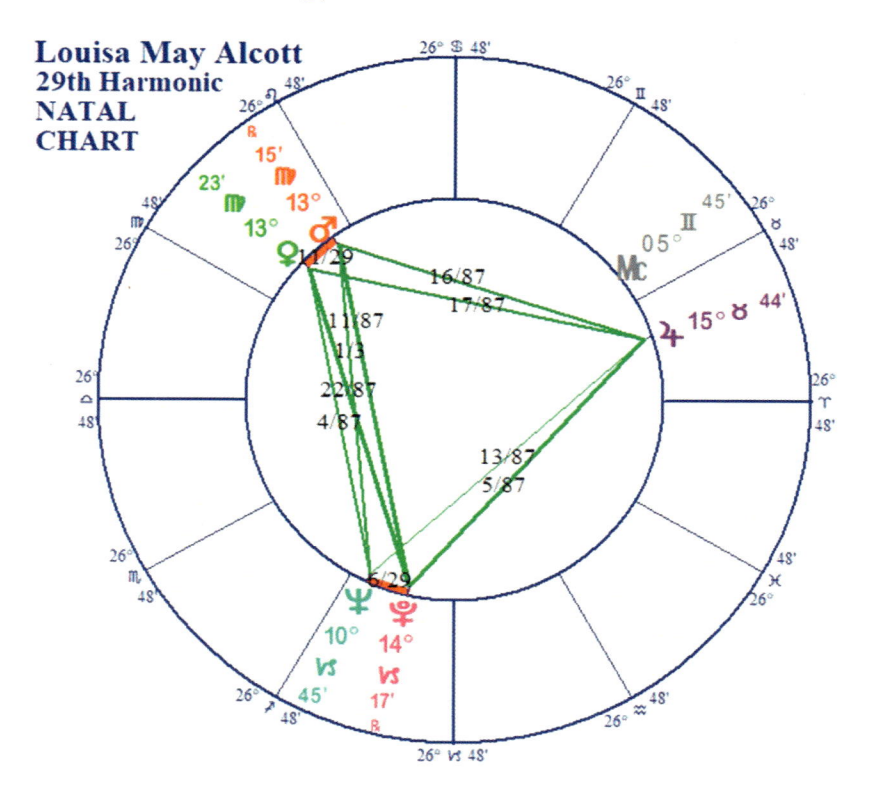

Aspects & Orbs

"**Spreading**" indicates aspects that are slightly or only minutes out of orb. These aspect circuits are weaker than when all aspects are in orb. **(Figure 21)**

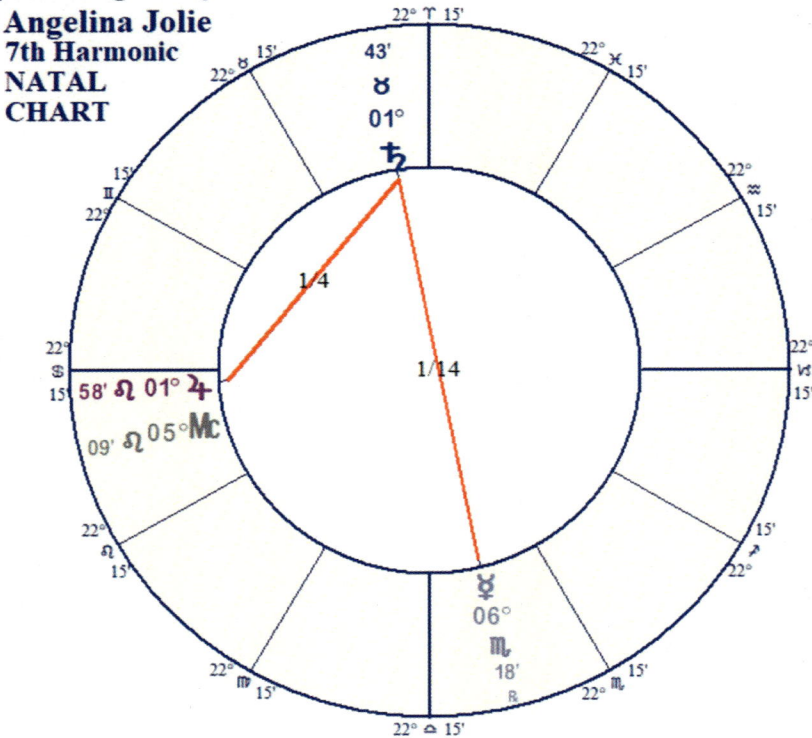

Figure 21: Spreading T-Square

In **Figure 21**, the T-Square is missing one Square aspect between Mercury and Jupiter. In this case, the planets are separated by 94°20'. The allowable orb in VA for a Square aspect is +or- 4°00' and a Square aspect is 90°. Since the separation is only minutes (0°20') out of orb, the aspect of Mercury, Saturn, Jupiter would be called a "Spreading T-Square".

Vibrational Astrology Study Guide Module One

I. Aspect Grids

The Aspect Grid provides information on the planetary aspects, either abbreviated or by symbol, with or without the degree of separation. It can be a table of supplementary information next to a chart wheel or a more-detailed grid is available as Special Charts. (Sirius: Right-click to access "Wheel Style", Click "Special", Select "H - Aspect Grids Only")

Because of the importance of the lower vibrations, many VA astrologers design their aspect grids to also show the 5-Vibe (Quintile), 7-Vibe (Septile), 9-Vibe (Novile), 11-Vibe (Unidecile), and 13-Vibe in color variations. In this way, they can see at a glance an increased number of planetary aspects in these vibrations. (**Figure 22**)

Figure 22: Aspect Grids (Ermete Zacconi)

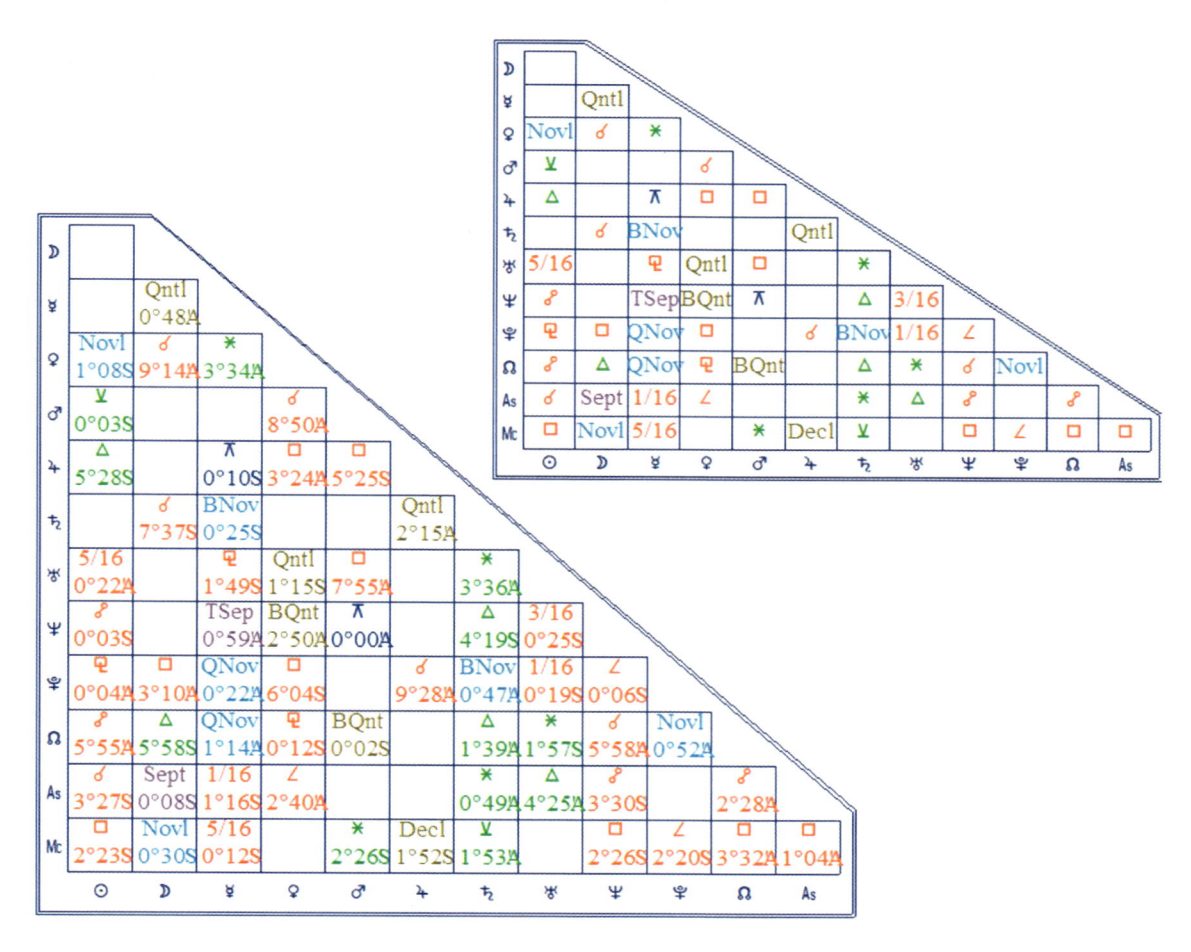

Aspects & Orbs

J. Summary: Aspects & Orbs

Ptolemaic aspects:
Conjunctions are adjacent to each other (0°) (Orb: 16°)
Oppositions are opposite each other (180°) (½) (Orb 8°)
Trine aspects have the same sign **Element (Fire, Earth, Air, Water)** (120°) (⅓) (Orb: 5°20') (4 signs apart)
Square aspects have the same sign **Mode (Cardinal, Fixed, Mutable)** (90°) (¼) (Orb: 4°) (3 signs apart)
Sextile aspects are in signs that are **two (2) signs apart** (60°) (⅙) (Orb: 2°40')

Elements: Fire Signs (Aries, Leo, Sagittarius)
Earth Signs (Taurus, Virgo, Capricorn)
Air Signs (Gemini, Libra, Aquarius)
Water Signs (Cancer, Scorpio, Pisces)

Modes: Cardinal Signs (Aries, Cancer, Libra and Capricorn)
Fixed Signs (Taurus, Leo, Scorpio, Aquarius)
Mutable Signs (Gemini, Virgo, Sagittarius, Pisces)

Ptolemaic aspects are identified by the aspect glyph in the Natal Chart. In the Vibrational Chart, the aspects may be identified by the element, mode, signs, line color, degrees of separation, and/or the glyph in the Aspect Grid.

Non-Ptolemaic Aspects:
Semisquare (45°) (⅛) (Orb: 2°)
Sesquiquadrate (135°) (⅜) (Orb: 2°)
Semisextile (30°) (1/12) (Orb: 1°20')
Quincunx (150°) (5/12) (Orb: 1°20')
1/16th Aspect (22.5°) (1/16) (Orb: 1°)

Non-Ptolemaic aspects are identified by the aspect glyph or a dashed aspect line in the Natal Chart. In the Vibrational Chart, the aspects may be identified by line color, a solid or dashed aspect line, degrees of separation, and/or glyph in the Aspect Grid.

Vibrational Astrology Study Guide Module One

Aspect interpretations:

Conjunction (0°) - Conjunctions involve planets that are adjacent to one another and get their meaning from the planets that aspect them. Combine their meanings with the vibration they occupy. They show the basic energy expressions and driving force in a person's life.

Opposition (180°) (½) - Oppositions create a polarity between the planets yielding an interest in sharing or conflicting with others

Square (90°) (1/4th) - Squares are a need to take action, providing the motivation and drive to do something, make changes, make progress or achieve a goal.

Trine (120°) (1/3rd) - Trines show unrestricted energy flow that is easy and tends to be smooth.

Sextile (60°) (1/6th) - Sextiles want to share in an easy, free-flowing manner.

Semisquare (45°) (1/8th) - Semisquares are what one has to do. They define one's mode of operation when one takes action.

Sesquiquadrate (135°) (3/8th) - Sesquiquadrates are similar to Semisquares except that they are more easily and naturally expressed and somewhat less stressful.

Semisextile (30°) (1/12th) - Semisextiles balance action and flow. They are a strongly ingrained quality.

Quincunx (150°) (5/12th) – Quincunxes represent energies that need to be developed. The vibration is the main descriptor of the growth needed with the two planets further refining the growth process. There is a strong motivation for these energies to grow into a useful mature behavior. If this growth process is unsuccessful then this trait will not be available in this vibration.

1/16, 3/16, 5/16, 7/16th Aspects (22.5°) (1/16th) - The 1/16th aspects indicate an action that originates in conscious internal processing that is not obvious to others. The 1/16th aspects are forming energy circuits; however, those circuits can be better understood by doubling the vibration.

Interpretation involves combining the meaning of the vibration with the meaning of the planets and aspects in the vibrational circuit.

Aspects & Orbs

Proportional Orbs:

An **orb** is the allowable difference between the planetary arc and the exact aspect.

Proportional orbs are required for the natal and vibrational aspects to parallel one another.

An aspect's strength is determined by the exactitude of the orb. The smaller the orb, the stronger the aspect, the larger the orb the weaker the aspect.

Proportional Orbs in VA:

Aspect	Orb
Conjunction	16°
Opposition	8°
Square	4°
Trine	5°20'
Sextile	2°40'
Semisquare	2°00'
Sesquiquadrate	2°00'
Semisextile	1°20'
Quincunx	1°20'
1/16th Aspect	1°00'

Vibrational Astrology Study Guide Module One

Aspect Rules:

Aspects in Vibrational Astrology require a third planet to complete an energetic circuit in each aspect configuration. Three or more planets connected through aspects require the application of the following rules to be read as energy circuits.

Settings for Aspect Lines:
Solid Red Lines: Conjunction, Opposition, Square, Semisquare, Sesquiquadrate
Dashed Red Lines: 1/16th aspects
Solid Green Lines: Trine, Sextile, and Semisextile
Solid Brown lines: Quincunx

Using the above criteria, the following rules for reading aspect energy flow apply:
    a. All planets (3 or more) connected by "Solid Red" aspect lines may be read.
    b. All planets (3 or more) connected by "Solid Green" aspect lines may be read.
    c. Combining Red and Green aspects: "Red" conjunction or opposition aspects combine with "Green" aspects when in a pattern of 3 or more planets

Active & Inactive Vibrational Circuits:

All aspect circuits of three planets or more in a vibration must have at least one fraction denominator on one of the aspect lines that is evenly divisible by the vibration to connect the circuit into that vibration and therefore be active in that vibration. If no aspect line denominators are evenly divisible by the vibration to connect the circuit into the vibration, that circuit is not active and cannot be read in that vibration.

Aspect Patterns in VA:

In VA, only five aspect patterns are identified by name: **Grand Trine, T-Square, Yod, Grand Cross,** and the **Kite**. All other patterns are described by the aspects composing the circuit.

Grand Trine: Three planets connected by Trine aspects (approximately 120° apart, within orb) in the same Element (Fire, Earth, Air, Water Signs)

T-Square: Three planets, two defined by an Opposition aspect with the third Squaring the two oppositional planets

Yod: Three planets connected by two Quincunxes and a Sextile

Grand Cross: Four planets all located approximately Square (approximately 90° apart, within orb), the Opposition planets creating a cross

Aspects & Orbs

Kite: Four planet aspect pattern composed of a Grand Trine with one planet opposite one of the points of the Grand Trine (all within orb) (Looks like a kite!)

"Power" aspect structure: The term, **"Power"**, preceding an aspect structure (or midpoint structure) describes a conjunction that adds an additional planet to the structure, thereby increasing the structure's significance in the life of the person.

"Double Power" aspect structure: The term, "Double Power", indicates the presence of two sets of conjunctions on different single planetary positions in a planetary structure.

"Spreading" indicates aspects that are slightly or only minutes out of orb. These aspect circuits are weaker than when all aspects are in orb.

Aspect Grids:
The **Aspect Grid** provides aspect information at a glance. In addition to the standard aspects normally shown, the VA astrologer often includes the Quintile (5-Vibe), Septile (7-Vibe), Novile (9-Vibe), 11-Vibe, and 13-Vibe for quick reference.

K. Books & Videos

Books

Berry, Linda & Cochrane, David, *Vibrational Astrology, Interpreting Aspects,* Gainesville: Cosmic Patterns Software, Inc., 2016. (Order through http://www.Lulu.com)

Cochrane, David, *Vibrational Astrology, the Essentials,* Gainesville, Florida: Cosmic Patterns Software, Inc, 2021

Videos
Astrology Tutorial Videos by David Cochrane
Https://www.astrologydc.com

Introduction to VA Course, Part 1
Mastering Astrology: Quickly identify Aspects, etc.
Identifying Aspects with Less than One Degree Orb in the Chart Wheel
Interpretation of Aspects to the Sun and Moon
Interpretation of Aspects of Planets to Mercury
Aspects of Outer Planets to Venus and Mars
Interpretation of Aspects Between the Outer Planets Jupiter to Pluto
Vibrational Charts (Intro to VA Course, Lesson 15)
VA Fundamentals in Detail, Part 1,2,3,4,5,6,7,8
VA Fundamentals in Detail, Part 1 Addendum

Aspects and Vibrational Charts
VA Fundamentals in Detail, Parts 1,2,3,4,5,6,7,8
Ptolemaic Aspects: A Test to See if they Work

Notes

CHAPTER 4: VA Vibration Interpretations (1-13)

   A. Introduction
   B. The First 13 Vibrations
   C. Summary: VA Vibration Energy Processes & Behaviors (1-13)
   D. Books & Videos

A. Introduction

Using Vibrational Astrology is like taking a microscope to a natal chart. Important patterns are revealed that would otherwise go unnoticed. Each vibrational chart expresses a specific meaning. Resonances of planetary combinations in the vibration are expressed within the context of the vibrational meaning.

Each vibrational chart is the natal chart focused on a particular vibration. The tightness of the orb in the aspect forming energy circuits indicates the strength of the vibration. In a vibration, when three or more planets strongly aspect one another, they become an active part of the person's energy structure. The planets serve the vibration, never overpowering it.

Vibrational Astrology is based on "extreme case sampling". This method of research evaluates biographical information from the strongest birth charts. Using a large database with a specific criterion and scoring system, a large number of charts are identified for evaluation. The research data was derived using research features in the Sirius 2.0 and 3.0 Astrology Software.

B. The First 13 Vibrations

A prime number or prime vibration is only *evenly* divisible by itself and the number one. Each prime number in a numerical sequence introduces a new behavioral characteristic. When a number is composed of more than one prime number, the result is a combination of the behavioral characteristics of the prime numbers involved. In the vibrational listing below, prime numbers have been underlined.

Following is a description of the first 13 vibrations. Vibrations 14-32 with primes to 59 will be discussed in Module 2, Chapter 6.

VA Vibration Interpretations (1-13)

The Natal Chart – This is the core energy from which the vibrational charts are derived. Tight aspect patterns in the natal chart will be active in several additional vibrations. Two planet aspects within one degree or 1/3rd of the allowable orb, whichever is smaller, may indicate a trait but not a behavior. The way these tight patterns manifest is seen in the vibrations where they form a strong energy circuit.

1-Vibration --

Energy Process: Using the internal sense of what is essential to the person to direct the life

Behavioral Symptoms: This is initially confusing because this chart is also the natal chart. It is read using VA vibrational chart methods when it contains significant conjunction patterns relative to other vibrational patterns. It refers to **self-directed behavior that is a fundamental characteristic of the person.** It shows a strong inclination to use one's internal way of thinking, sensing, and operating as an underlying and perhaps exclusive determiner of one's behavior. It shows the extent to which one is self-referenced rather than other-referenced. One tends to rely on one's intuition, knowledge, experience, and creations as the foundation reference points for living one's life. There may be a strong sense of what one's innate talents are and what one's life path is from an early age.

Derivation: The natal Conjunction

2-Vibration --

Energy Process: Polarized interaction/exchange with something outside yourself

Behavioral Symptoms: The 2-Vibration opens one physically and emotionally to that which surrounds them. It is the extension of internal self-awareness outward into awareness of the world around one. It includes **how we interact with each other, how we share with and/or oppose others.**

Derivation: The natal **Opposition** (1/2 of 360° or 180°) is a conjunction in the 2-Vibration. Two is a prime number.

3-Vibration --
Energy Process: Free unrestricted smooth flow of energy
Behavioral Symptoms: The 3-Vibration **represents an easy flow between the planets involved.** The talents and capabilities originating from this easy flow tend to be taken for granted because they are experienced as being so easy, smooth, and natural that there is no struggle involved. There may, however, be discomfort if the two energies combined in the trine operate very differently. Additionally, when three planets are in a Grand Trine with tight orbs, midpoint structures are formed, and this more challenging energy is likely to be used in the structuring of life.
Derivation: The natal **Trine** (1/3 of 360° or 120°) is a conjunction in the 3-Vibration. Three is a prime number.

4-Vibration --
Energy Process: A need rising from within that shapes what one is driven to do
Behavioral Symptoms: The 4-Vibration becomes **motivation and drive to have an impact and to change circumstances.** Four is very focused on its motivations and drive to accomplish without considering the motives and drives of others or their opinions of its actions. Square aspects in natal charts are not as difficult to deal with as they are by transit or progression.
Derivation: The natal **Square** (1/4 of 360° or 90°) is a conjunction in the 4-Vibration. Four is the square of 2.

VA Vibration Interpretations (1-13)

5-Vibration --
Energy Process: An organic exploration and interaction that is nonlinear and outwardly directed.
Behavioral Symptoms: The 5-Vibration involves a **natural process of exploration.** This process often results in understanding patterns and how things connect. And it is **often experienced as a joyful play and satisfying creative discovery.** This nonlinear exploration process is different for everyone. When the orbs are small, these planets and aspects create the fundamental energy flow that is obvious in the person's life.

People with a strong 5-Vibration tend to remove themselves from stressful, demanding situations. As a result, they tend to avoid the stress of high success. They are often more competent than their level of success in the world indicates. If they do achieve a high level of success, they tend to do it without the struggle that others must endure. Success occurs due to being in the right place at the right time, not through the stress of operating out of a strong inner drive.
Derivation: The natal **Quintile** (1/5 of 360° or 72°) and the other 5ths of the circle are conjunctions in the 5-Vibration. Five is a prime number and introduces a new fundamental way of operating.

6-Vibration --
Energy Process: A free flow of interactive energy
Behavioral Symptoms: The 6-Vibration **wants to share with others in a free-flowing manner.** This usually results in people interacting with each other in caring, harmonious ways.
Derivation: The natal **Sextile** (1/6 of 360° or 60°) is a conjunction in the 6-Vibration. This is a combination of vibrations two and three. The "three" (trine) is free-flowing energy. By itself, the trine does not need to share. By adding the polarity of the "two" (opposition), the person does need to share with others and a new meaning arises.

Copyright © The Avalon School of Astrology, Inc. All Rights Reserved
All chart wheels and reports used in this module are created from Sirius 3.0 with permission from Cosmic Patterns Software.

7-Vibration --

Energy Process: Quieting, internalizing, deepening one's energy, and formulating internal understandings

Behavioral Symptoms: The 7-Vibration is **quiet, introverted, deep, and profound.** It slows and quiets the individual, enabling them to internalize and process their experiences in a deep, profound way. Seven Vibration looks for and needs to develop a deeper understanding. It appreciates and seeks mastery. The internal focus of Seven results in **intense concentration and self-discipline.** Sustained attention, focus, and repetition of practice enable it to develop skill and awareness and these individuals often become masters themselves. It tends to **form its own internal reality or way of visualizing and understanding life.** The understanding can be in abstract or **symbolic thinking.** 7-Vibration may become exceptional in many different areas. Some of these are athletics, music, arts, and sciences.

Derivation: The natal **Septile** (1/7 of 360° or approximately 51.4°) and the other 7ths of the circle are conjunctions in the 7-Vibration. Seven is a prime and introduces a new behavior pattern.

8-Vibration --

Energy Process: Action that makes a difference

Behavioral Symptoms: The 8-Vibration **engages in concrete actions that manifest results.** This energy is a fundamental part of the person and is expressed in a direct, strong way. It shows one's characteristic way of interfacing with the world. The nature of the actions will be determined by the planets & aspect patterns involved.

Derivation: The natal **Semisquare** (1/8 of 360° or 45°) and the natal **Sesquiquadrate** (3/8 of 360° or 135°) are conjunctions in the 8-Vibration. The 4-Vibration is the motivation and drive that pushes you toward action, and the 8-Vibration is the next octave, actually taking the actions needed to bring about manifestation.

9-Vibration --

Energy Process: The process of integration and bonding with the environment

Behavioral Symptoms: The 9-Vibration flows outward merging with the individual's environment, family, and people in their neighborhood and community. This is not necessarily a matter of location. A community can be a group of people that share a common interest or that interact regularly located all over the world. Persons with a strong 9-Vibration **deal with areas of integration, and connectedness to their eclectic group or circle.** It influences how one relates in a shared environment and the way the community perceives one. This harmonic **has a healing, soothing quality that can bring wholeness and a feeling of contentment.** When Neptune is focused in the 9-Vibration, it wants to heal and uplift those around it. When Uranus is focused in the 9-Vibration, it tends to operate with an awareness of community cycles and rhythms.

Derivation: The natal **Novile** (1/9 of 360° or 40°) and the other 9ths of the circle are conjunctions in the 9-Vibration. Nine is 3 to the second power (squared). The easy internal flow of three becomes a flow with the individual's environment,

Note: The essential vibrations for psychological health are the 5-, 7- and 9-Vibrations. The development of at least one of these opens the door to developing higher vibrations.

10-Vibration --

Energy Process: Organic exploration and interaction that is shared with others

Behavioral Symptoms: In the 10-Vibration, **non-linear, organic exploration, interaction, play, and creativity are shared with others.** For 10-Vibration, shared creative play is more pleasurable and a strong 10-Vibration is more apt to engage freely in creating a shared experience.

Derivation: The natal **Decile** (1/10 of 360° or 36°) and the other 10ths of the circle are conjunctions in the 10-Vibration. Ten is 5x2. Thus, it combines the organic creativity and play of 5 with the interactiveness of 2.

Vibrational Astrology Study Guide Module One

11-Vibration --

Energy Process: Restless, dissatisfied, reaching out for something more or different, desires change.

Behavioral Symptoms: The 11-Vibration is **restless in the present circumstances** and always seeking something more, something different. Thus, it **tends to be progressive. It Is easily bored and needs ongoing stimulation**. 11-Vibration may also be unstable. Strong aspects can sometimes be related to psychological problems.

The eleventh vibration is inclined to music because as soon as one plays or sings one note, one must move to the next one. Musicians tend to have aspects such as Venus-Saturn and Venus-Uranus in the 11-Vibration more than other professions. Rock and roll musicians tend to have Venus-Uranus-Pluto combined in the 11-Vibration. With strong 11-Vibrations, music or dance can be recommended as an activity that can be helpful to a person not handling their 11-Vibration well.

Derivation: The natal **Unidecile** (1/11 of 360° or approximately 32.7°) and the other 11ths of the circle are conjunctions in the 11-Vibration. 11 is a prime number.

12-Vibration --

Energy Process: Seeks to balance the push outward of motivation and drive, with receptivity that is coming in so that there is an easy flow between yourself and others

Behavioral Symptoms: The 12-Vibration seeks a balance point within the process of giving and receiving. It is as if one were combining yin and yang. **A gentle, smooth flowing receptivity is operating in union with an outward movement that is conveying one's motivations and drives. The motivation and drive must be expressed in a way that generates a smooth harmonious interaction with others.**

This can be an ongoing developmental process. The Quincunx seems to be a potential way of balancing receptivity and motivation that is difficult to initially get in touch with. It develops throughout life. Eventually, it can become a dominant part of the way one deals with life.

Derivation: The natal **Semisextile** (1/12 of 360° or 30°) and the natal **Quincunx** (5/12 of 360° or 150°) are conjunctions in the 12-Vibration. Twelve is 3x4 and 2x6. Thus, it is a combination of the easy flow of 3 and the motivation and drives of 4, combined with the awareness of 2 that there is something besides me that I need to interact with and the expression of 6 in a smooth and easy flowing, harmonious manner.

13-Vibration --
Energy Process: Going deep within, seeking to uncover one's distinct essence and make it the new operating center of life

Behavioral Symptoms: The 13-Vibration **has the drive to move beyond the average and the mediocre. There is an inherent need to discover a special or exceptional essence that is deeply felt and a willingness to work hard to find and connect with this essence.** Thirteen trusts its own internal experience of being special and is not likely to seek input from others or consider the opinions of others. Expressing its individuality in a special and unique way is fundamental to its identity. It tends to feel a sense of mission or purpose connected with this special awareness and talents found within. There is the potential for an inner paradigm shift that brings dramatic changes in thinking or behavior and perhaps a sense of transcendence.

A person with a strong 13-Vibration may have heroes or idols that they perceive as having connected into that special unique core essence within. And Thirteen seeks to learn from them how to make that same inner connection. The following of a guru is an example. Sometimes these people feel entitled. You may see this with criminals. They do not feel the need to follow other people's laws. In general, thirteen tends to have a sense of entitlement and freedom that results in them going their own way.

Derivation: The natal thirteenths (1/13 of 360° or approximately 27.7°) and the other 13ths of the circle are conjunctions in the 13-Vibration. Thirteen is a prime number.

Vibrational Astrology Study Guide Module One

C. Summary: VA Vibrations: Energy Processes & Behaviors (1-13)

A summarization of the energy processes and behavioral symptoms of vibrations one through thirteen are listed below. With each prime number in the vibrational sequence, a new behavioral characteristic(s) is introduced. **Vibrations of <u>Prime Numbers</u> are highlighted and underlined below.**

<u>The Natal Chart – A combination of all the potential vibrations of the person, the life's patterns in all their complexity.</u>

Keywords or "catch phrases", listed below, are provided in parentheses in red as a reminder or trigger for the basic meanings or behaviors of the first 13 vibrations.

<u>1-Vibration</u> - (Self)
  Energy: Using the internal sense of what is essential to the person to direct the life
  Note: The 1-Vibration is read as a vibrational chart only when it contains significant conjunction patterns relative to the other vibrational charts.
  Behavior: Self-directed behavior is a fundamental characteristic of the person

<u>2-Vibration</u> – (Polarity, Sharing)
  Energy: Polarized interaction/exchange with something outside yourself
  Behavior: How we interact with each other, how we share and/or oppose others.

<u>3-Vibration</u> - (Smooth & Harmonious)
  Energy: Free, unrestricted, smooth flow of energy
  Behavior: Represents an easy flow between the planets involved

4-Vibration - (Motivation & Drive)
  Energy: A need rising from within that shapes what one is driven to do
  Behavior: Motivation & drive to have an impact and to change circumstances

<u>5-Vibration</u> - (Playfulness & Creativity)
  Energy: An organic exploration and interaction that is nonlinear and outwardly directed
  Behavior: Natural process of exploration; often experienced as joyful play and satisfying creative discovery

Copyright © The Avalon School of Astrology, Inc. All Rights Reserved
All chart wheels and reports used in this module are created from Sirius 3.0 with permission from Cosmic Patterns Software

VA Vibration Interpretations (1-13)

6-Vibration – (Harmonious Interaction with Others)
Energy: The free flow of interactive energy
Behavior: Wants to share with others in a free-flowing manner

7-Vibration – (Quiet, Meditative, Introverted)
Energy: Quieting, internalizing, deepening one's energy, and formulating internal understandings
Behavior: Quiet, introverted, deep and profound; has intense concentration and self-discipline; forms own internal world, may utilize abstract or symbolic thinking

8-Vibration - (Action)
Energy: Action that makes a difference
Behavior: Engages in a concrete action that manifests results

9-Vibration – (Integration & Bonding; Healing & Soothing)
Energy: The process of integration and bonding with the environment
Behavior: Deals with areas of integration, and connectedness to one's eclectic group or circle; Has a healing, soothing quality that can bring wholeness and a feeling of contentment

Note: 5-, 7-, and 9-Vibrations are essential for psychological health. The development of at least one of these opens the door to developing higher vibrations.

10-Vibration - (Play and Creative Expression with Others)
Energy: Organic exploration and interaction that is shared with others
Behavior: Engages in shared experiences of interaction, organic exploration, play, and creativity

11-Vibration – (Progressive, Restless, Hungry for Change)
Energy: Restless, dissatisfied, reaching out for something more or different, desires change
Behavior: Restless and dissatisfied with the present circumstances; tends to be progressive; seeks something new or different; tends to be easily bored and needs stimulation

Copyright © The Avalon School of Astrology, Inc. All Rights Reserved
All chart wheels and reports used in this module are created from Sirius 3.0 with permission from Cosmic Patterns Software.

12-Vibration – (Combines Challenging & Dynamic with Free-flowing)
  Energy: Seeks to balance the push outward of motivation and drive, with receptivity that is coming in so that there is an easy flow between yourself and others
  Behavior: A gentle, smooth flowing receptivity is operating in union with an outward movement that is conveying one's motivations and drives. The motivation and drive must be expressed in a way that generates a smooth harmonious interaction with others.

13-Vibration – (Moves Beyond Average or Mediocre)
  Energy: Going within, seeking to uncover one's distinct essence and make it the new operating center of life
  Behavior: Has a drive to move beyond the average and mediocre; An inherent need to discover a special or exceptional essence that is deeply felt and a willingness to work hard to find and connect with this essence.

Summary of "catch phrases" for Vibrations 1-13:
1-Vibration – Self
2-Vibration – Polarity, Sharing
3-Vibration – Smooth & Harmonious
4-Vibration – Motivation & Drive
5-Vibration – Playfulness & Creativity
6-Vibration – Harmonious Interaction with Others
7-Vibration – Quiet, Meditative, Introverted
8-Vibration – Action
9-Vibration – Integration & Bonding; Healing & Soothing
10-Vibration – Play & Creative Expression with Others
11-Vibration – Progressive, Restless Hungry for Change
12-Vibration – Combines Challenging & Dynamic with Free-flowing
13-Vibration – Moves Beyond Average or Mediocre

VA Vibration Interpretations (1-13)

D. Books & Videos

Books

Berry, Linda & Cochrane, David, *Vibrational Astrology, Interpreting Aspects,* Gainesville: Cosmic Patterns Software, inc., 2016. (Order through http://www.Lulu.com)

Cochrane, David, *Vibrational Astrology, the Essentials,* Gainesville, Florida: Cosmic Patterns Software, Inc, 2021

Videos
Astrology Tutorial Videos by David Cochrane
Https://www.astrologydc.com

Introduction to VA Course, Part 1
Introducing Meanings of Vibrations
Meanings of Harmonics 1 to 8
Meanings of Harmonics 9 to 16

Aspects and Vibrational Charts
Meanings of Harmonics 1 to 8
Meanings of Harmonics 9 to 16

Notes

NOTES

Vibrational Astrology Study Guide Module One

CHAPTER 5: Basic VA Chart Interpretation

A. What is a Vibrational Chart?
B. Proportional Orbs and Aspect Color Settings
C. Midpoint Patterns
   1. Midpoint Settings in VA
   2. Evaluating Midpoint Orbs
   3. Midpoints
   4. Isotraps
   5. Midpoint Isotraps
D. How to Read an Astrology Chart Using VA
   1. Confirm the Birth Information & Source
   2. Natal Chart
   3. Midpoint Patterns
   4. Harmonic Listing #8
   5. Harmonic Listing #1
   6. Vibrations for Beginning Astrological Screening
   7. Aspect Pattern Review
E. Summary: Basic VA Chart Interpretation
F. Books & Videos

A. What is a Vibrational Chart?

VA is based on the assumption that non-Ptolemaic aspects, historically known as minor aspects, are as important as Ptolemaic aspects. However, it is difficult to identify non-Ptolemaic aspects in a natal chart.

Vibrational charts are derived from the natal chart. VA uses mathematical calculations to reveal powerful aspects beyond the Ptolemaic aspects. The Vibrational Charts reveal the depth and complexity in the astrology chart. Thus, Vibrational Astrology describes the person, their motivations and talents, their way of life, and who they are in precise detail.

To understand a vibrational chart, the following points are important:

a. An aspect is a fraction of a circle. (Trine = $\frac{1}{3}$, Square = $\frac{1}{4}$, Quintile=$\frac{1}{5}$, Biquintile=$\frac{2}{5}$, etc.)
b. The meaning of an aspect is in the fraction: the numerator (top) and the denominator (bottom)

Basic VA Chart Interpretation

    c. The denominator is much more important than the numerator. The denominator shows the "vibration". For example, the ⅛ (Semisquare) and the ⅜ (Sesquiquadrate) aspects are 8-Vibration aspects and will be conjunct in that vibration.
    d. All aspects with the same denominator have a similar meaning.

B. Proportional Orbs and Aspect Color Settings

Proportional orbs are used to parallel the natal aspects in the vibrational charts. The aspect orbs for vibrational charts are shown in **Figure 1**.

Figure 1: Proportional Orbs in VA

Aspect	Orb	Calculation
Conjunction (0°)	16°	(16/1)
Opposition (180°)	8°	(16/2)
Square (90°)	4°	(16/4)
Trine (120°)	5°20'	(16/3)
Sextile (60°)	2°40'	(16/6)
Semisquare (45°)	2°00'	(16/8)
Sesquiquadrate (135°)	2°00'	(16/8)
Semisextile (30°)	1°20'	(16/12)
Quincunx (150°)	1°20'	(16/12)
1/16th Aspect (22.5°)	1°00'	(16/16)

Set aspect orbs as indicated above and colors as follows:
Solid Red lines: Conjunction, Opposition, Square, Semisquare, Sesquiquadrate
Dashed Red lines: 1/16th Aspect
Solid Green lines: Trine, Sextile and Semisextile
Solid Brown lines: Quincunx

Vibrational Astrology Study Guide Module One

C. Midpoint Patterns

Midpoint Structures were popularized by astrologer Reinhold Ebertin in the mid to late 20th century. Ebertin called his system of astrology, Cosmobiology. In Vibrational Astrology, David Cochrane extended Ebertin's work with midpoints.

VA only uses conjunctions and oppositions for Midpoint analysis. Planetary Midpoint Structures utilize a maximum orb of 1°30' in all charts, natal and vibrational.

VA does not use the angles, the Ascendent (ASC) and Midheaven (MC), in Midpoint Structures in natal charts or their vibrations as the exact positions of the angles are unknown. The position of the angles changes if the birth time is even 5 or 10 minutes off. In charts with exact times, such as a New Moon chart, the ASC and MC locations are known and can be used in chart interpretations. Both the ASC and MC are powerful points and useful when an accurate time is known.

1. Midpoint Settings in VA

In Sirius Astrology Software, the Midpoint Settings Screen is accessed as follows:
1. In Menu Bar, Select "Listing"
2. Click "Midpoints"
3. Select "Midpoints (View/Change Settings first)"
4. Set Midpoint Settings screen as shown in **Figure 2.**
    a. On the left, Check 'Print Midpoint Trees";
    b. On the left, "Aspects in Midpoint Trees:", Check only the "Conjunction & Opposition" aspect; Change the deg-min setting to 1 Deg 30 Min.
    c. On the right, under "Midpoint Listings" establish a 180- or 360- Degree Sort and verify that line is checked.
    d. On the bottom right, Check "Save these setting as new default"
5. Click "OK"

Basic VA Chart Interpretation

Figure 2: Midpoint (View/Change Settings First) Screen

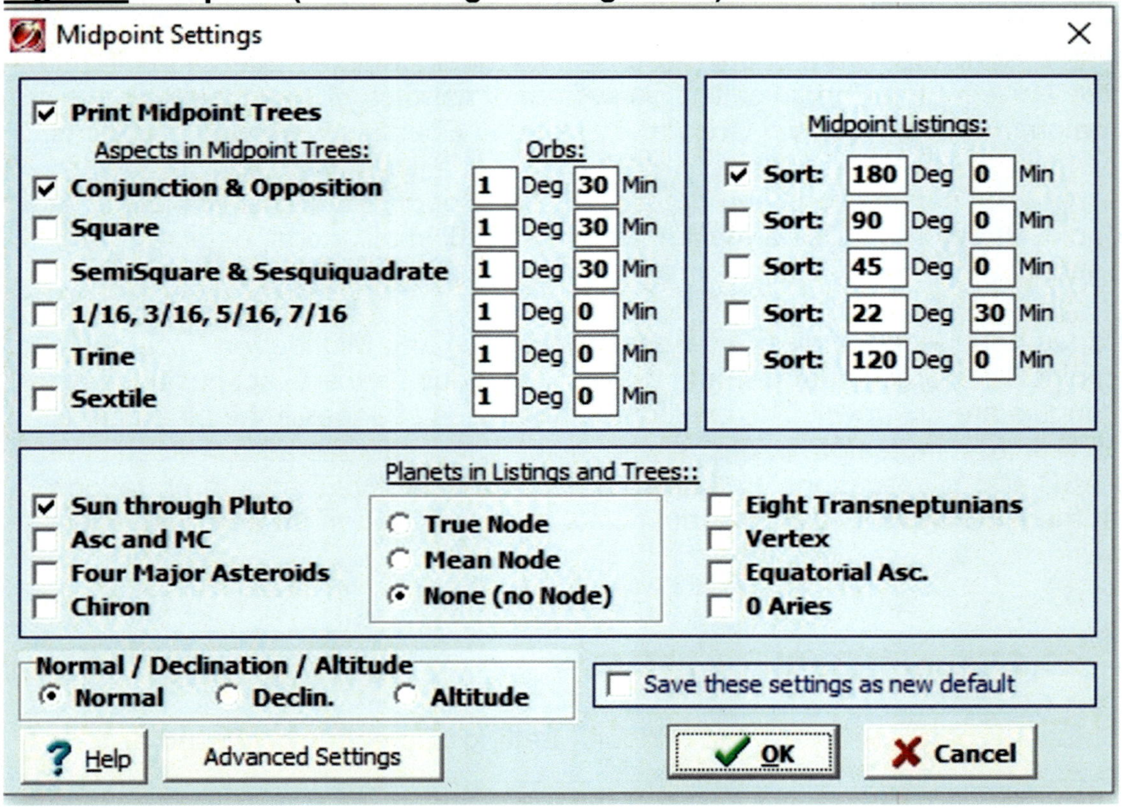

[Screenshot of Midpoint Settings dialog box with the following options:

Print Midpoint Trees ✓
Aspects in Midpoint Trees: — Orbs:
- ✓ Conjunction & Opposition — 1 Deg 30 Min
- ☐ Square — 1 Deg 30 Min
- ☐ SemiSquare & Sesquiquadrate — 1 Deg 30 Min
- ☐ 1/16, 3/16, 5/16, 7/16 — 1 Deg 0 Min
- ☐ Trine — 1 Deg 0 Min
- ☐ Sextile — 1 Deg 0 Min

Midpoint Listings:
- ✓ Sort: 180 Deg 0 Min
- ☐ Sort: 90 Deg 0 Min
- ☐ Sort: 45 Deg 0 Min
- ☐ Sort: 22 Deg 30 Min
- ☐ Sort: 120 Deg 0 Min

Planets in Listings and Trees::
- ✓ Sun through Pluto
- ☐ Asc and MC
- ☐ Four Major Asteroids
- ☐ Chiron
- ☐ True Node
- ☐ Mean Node
- ● None (no Node)
- ☐ Eight Transneptunians
- ☐ Vertex
- ☐ Equatorial Asc.
- ☐ 0 Aries

Normal / Declination / Altitude
● Normal ☐ Declin. ☐ Altitude

☐ Save these settings as new default

[Help] [Advanced Settings] [OK] [Cancel]]

Following the setup, Click "Listing", "Midpoints", "Midpoints" to access the Midpoint Tree and Listing Screen. Or click the green square icon "MPT".

2. Evaluating Midpoint Orbs

The Midpoint Orb range is 0°00' to 1°30'. The smaller the orb, the stronger the Midpoint Structure. Very close orbs (less than 0°15') represent the strong life impacts. Very wide orbs (up to 1°30') reflect possible internal traits. These midpoints are not always active. Chapter 5, page 90, describes methods of midpoint activation.

Midpoint evaluation:

    a. Midpoint Structures <u>less than 0°15'</u> will show prominently in the person's life.

    b. Midpoint Structures <u>greater than 0°15' and less than 0°30'</u> that include an inner planet are STRONG. An orb less than 0°30' is so powerful, it will be a major theme in the person's life. 80-90% of the time, they can identify with it. If they do not, something is blocking it.

    c. Midpoint Structures <u>greater than 0°30' and less than 1°</u> have a noticeable impact if those same planets involved are also in an aspect. Whenever the planets in any Midpoint Structure are also in an aspect in the chart wheel, that combination is much stronger.

    d. Midpoint Structures <u>greater than 1° and less than 1°30'</u> are not as strong with planetary characteristics, only slightly visible.

    e. A 4-5+ activated planet midpoint pattern will be very significant in the life of the person.

Basic VA Chart Interpretation

3. Midpoints

A **Midpoint** is a point halfway between two planets.

A **Focal Point** is a point that is conjunct or opposite the midpoint of two other planets.

A **Focal Planet** is a planet located at the focal point, conjunct or opposite the midpoint of two other planets. In the midpoint listing in **Figure 3,** Moon, Venus, Jupiter, Uranus, and Pluto are all focal planets.

A **Slash (/)** indicates the midpoint. In other systems of astrology, the slash may be used loosely to mean any combination of planets. This is incorrect and unacceptable in VA because "/" always means Midpoint.

"=" or "AT" indicates a planet is conjunct or opposite the midpoint of two other planets. (Example: Sun = Moon/Saturn (written form) but we may say, "The Sun is AT the Moon/Saturn midpoint," referencing either a conjunction or an opposition.) In reality, whether it is a conjunction or opposition will make very little difference in the interpretation. The aspect glyphs are only used to make it clear (recommended).

A **Parentheses "(AND ")"** indicates planets that are working together: "(Sun opp Mercury) = Moon/Mars". If no aspect is shown, then a conjunction is assumed: "(Sun Mercury) = Moon/Mars".

A **Midpoint Structure** is formed when one planet (focal planet) is conjunct or opposite the midpoint of two planets. The terms, **Near Midpoint** (conjunction) and **Far Midpoint** (opposition), are used to differentiate between the two forms of Midpoint Structures. **(Figure 3)** Near and Far Midpoints have the same orb since it is the distance from the **Line of Symmetry** passing through the conjunction and opposition midpoints that is important.

A **Midpoint Axis**, **Symmetry Axis** or **Line of Symmetry** is the line between the conjunction (near) midpoint and opposition (far) midpoint of the midpoint structure.

A **Tight Midpoint Structure** indicates a midpoint structure with a very small orb (0-20 minutes).

A **Strong Midpoint Structure** is synonymous with a Tight Midpoint Structure, but its meaning is less clear. The astrology of a "strong midpoint structure" may take into account additional considerations, such as the focal planet is almost exactly on an angular house cusp or some other planetary, nodal, or asteroid relationship.

A **Weak Midpoint Structure** occurs when the orb of the midpoint structure is relatively large and not part of a large midpoint tree. In VA, a weak midpoint structure would have an orb greater than 1°15' or 1°20'.

Surrounding Planets references the two planets surrounding the focal planet in a Midpoint Structure.

A **Midpoint Tree** is a diagram that shows a focal planet with one or more midpoint structures. **(Figure 3)**

A **Resonance (res)** occurs when the angular distances between pairs of planets match or are within orb. This creates an energy activation in the same way that striking one tuning fork will cause another in the same room to vibrate. In resonances, the energetic stimulation of one of the pairs of planets will also stimulate the second pair of planets.

Resonances have to be stimulated to vibrate. When they are stimulated, the resonance provides a delicacy, a sensitivity, an ability to work with fine details. This enables the midpoint pattern to express itself with refinement and finesse that is not available in an aspect circuit.

A **Midpoint Resonance** is a single midpoint structure composed of either a near or far midpoint having one resonance. The Near and Far Midpoint Structures in **Figure 3** each have one **Resonance**. A Midpoint Tree has varying resonances.

There are several ways to activate a resonance:
1. Within the vibration, a planetary circuit (or aspected pair of planets) involving the planets in the midpoint will be an ongoing activation of that midpoint.
2. A conjunction of the three planets in a related vibration.
3. Another person's chart can activate the midpoint.
4. Transits and Progressions can temporarily activate the midpoint
5. Once the midpoint is activated the person may well continue to use it, providing mental stimulation of their own to resonate with it.

Through conscious awareness and intention, it is possible to sense and use the energies of midpoints more fully. Once the midpoint is identified and incorporated into one's personal structure, one can maintain its resonance through conscious use, taking full advantage of its gift in one's life.

Vibrational Astrology Study Guide Module One

Figure 3: Midpoint Structures & Midpoint Tree

Robert Haack
NATAL CHART Tropical/Equal

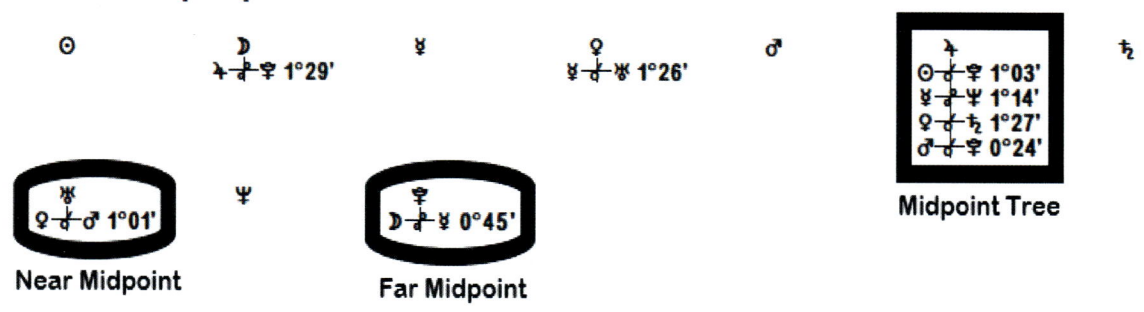

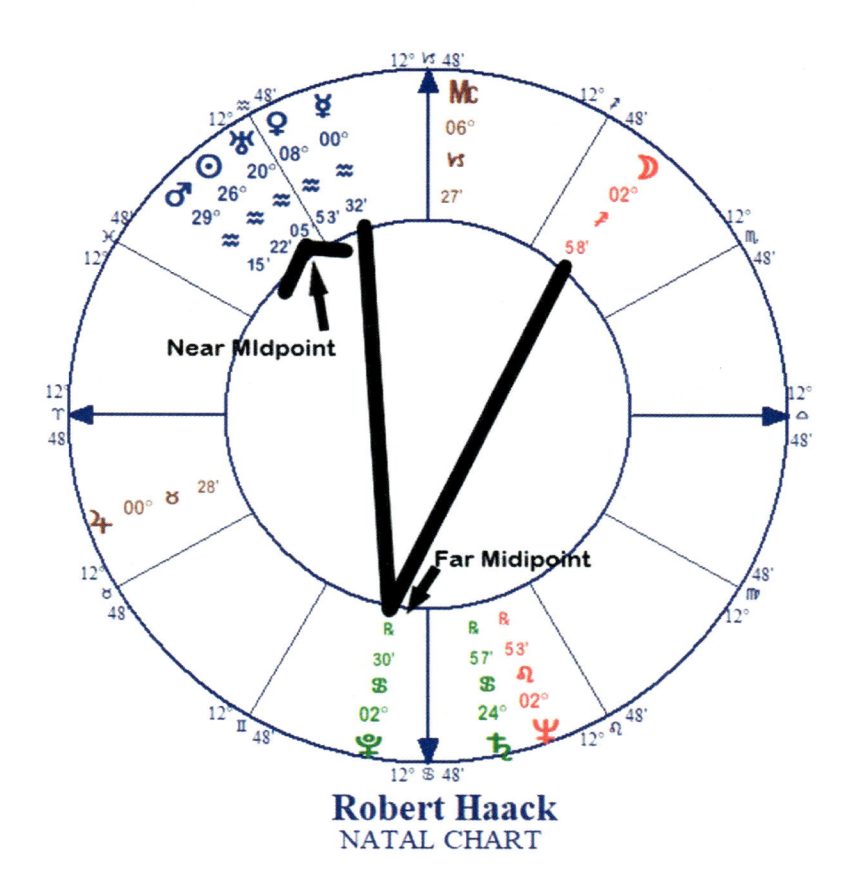

☉   ☽ ♃-♄-♇ 1°29'   ☿   ♀ ☿-♅ 1°26'   ♂   **♃**
                                              ☉-♂-♇ 1°03'
                                              ☿-♂-♆ 1°14'
                                              ♀-♂-♄ 1°27'
                                              ♂-♂-♇ 0°24'
                                              Midpoint Tree   ♄

♅   ♆   **♇**
♀-♂-♂ 1°01'   ☽-♂-☿ 0°45'

Near Midpoint   **Far Midpoint**

Robert Haack
NATAL CHART

Basic VA Chart Interpretation

Power Midpoint Structure is a midpoint structure where one of the planets forms a conjunction with another planet and both are within orb. **(Figure 4)** In the Midpoint Trees in **Figure 4**, one of the planets is duplicated in the Midpoint Structure. This indicates that one of the Surrounding Planets in the Midpoint Structure forms a conjunction with another planet that is within orb of the Focal Planet.

The **Power Midpoint Structure** has three (3) resonances as a result of the conjunction. In the case of Moon opposite Nep/SunPlu in **Figure 4**, Moon-Sun res Moon-Nep, Moon-Nep res Moon-Plu, and Moon-Sun res Moon-Plu comprise the resonances.

Also in **Figure 4**, in the **Power Midpoint Structure** of Sat conjunct Jup/SunPlu, Sat-Sun res Sat-Jup, Sat-Jup res Sat-Plu, and Sat-Sun res Sat-Plu comprise the 3 resonances.

Figure 4: Power Midpoint Structure

92
Copyright © The Avalon School of Astrology, Inc. All Rights Reserved
All chart wheels and reports used in this module are created from Sirius 3.0 with permission from Cosmic Patterns Software.

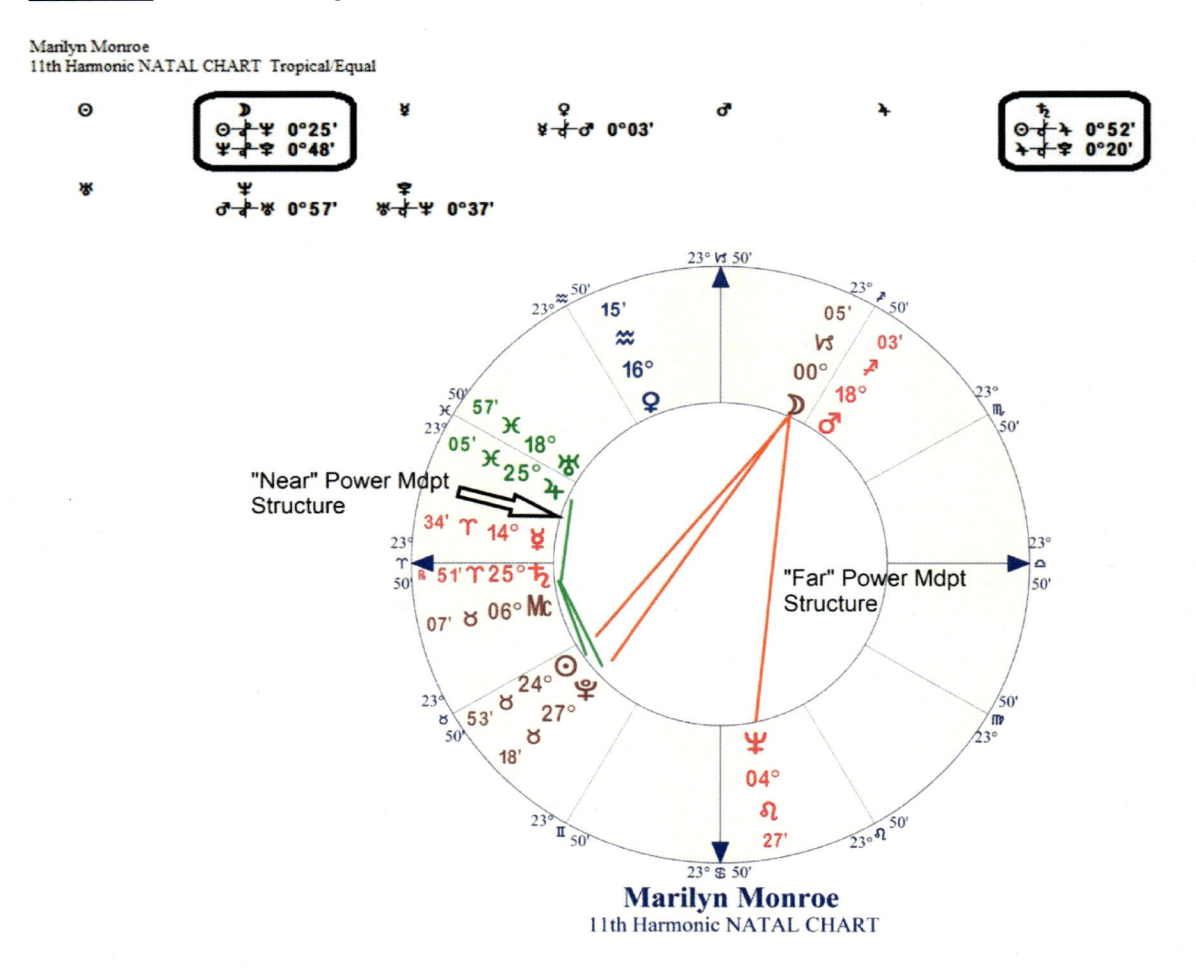

Direct Midpoint Structure is synonymous with **Midpoint Structure**. It indicates there is a focal point planet conjunct or opposite to the midpoint. Sirius Software occasionally uses the term Direct Midpoint Structure to specify the type of report for astrologers unfamiliar with VA.

Indirect Midpoint Structures refer to planets making aspects other than conjunction or opposition to the midpoint of two other planets. These midpoint aspects are **NOT** used in VA.

How to interpret a midpoint structure: Focus on the planet in the middle and connect to the energy of the two planets that produce the midpoint. Simply combine the planetary meanings. With multiple midpoints, combine in decreasing order of strength, strongest first.

Basic VA Chart Interpretation

4. Isotraps

An **Isotrap (Figure 5)** is a shortened term for an Isosceles Trapezoid. There are three ways to describe an isotrap.
- It is two pairs of planets that are separated by nearly the same angular distance. No planet is positioned at the midpoint.
- It is a four (4) planet pattern in which the midpoint of two of the planets is conjunct or opposite the midpoint of the other two planets.
- Another term for conjunct or opposite the same midpoint is a **Midpoint-to-Midpoint Alignment or Midpoint Alignment**.
- Note: All four planets must be different.

The terms, **Alignment and Aligned**, are used to indicate planets that are in conjunction or opposition with one another or on an axis.

A **Midpoint or Symmetry Axis** is a **line of symmetry** crossing both the near and far planetary midpoints. In **Figure 5**, the line bisecting the top and bottom of the Isotrap (lines B & D) form the **Midpoint or Symmetry Axis**.

In an exact Isotrap, the center line or **Midpoint Axis** in **Figure 5** would create exact mirror images. The sides (A&C) would be of equal length and the diagonals (E&F) would be equal in length. As a result, the base angles would be identical. The equal sides (A=C) and equal diagonals (E=F) of the isotrap **create the two resonances**. When an isotrap is not exact, the sides and diagonals are close to the same length but not equal, however, they must be within orb for this to be an isotrap.

The terms "Symmetry" and "Resonance" are fundamental principles in areas of science such as quantum physics and they are fundamental in Vibrational Astrology as well.

Vibrational Astrology Study Guide Module One

Figure 5: Isotrap (2 Resonances: A res C and E res F)

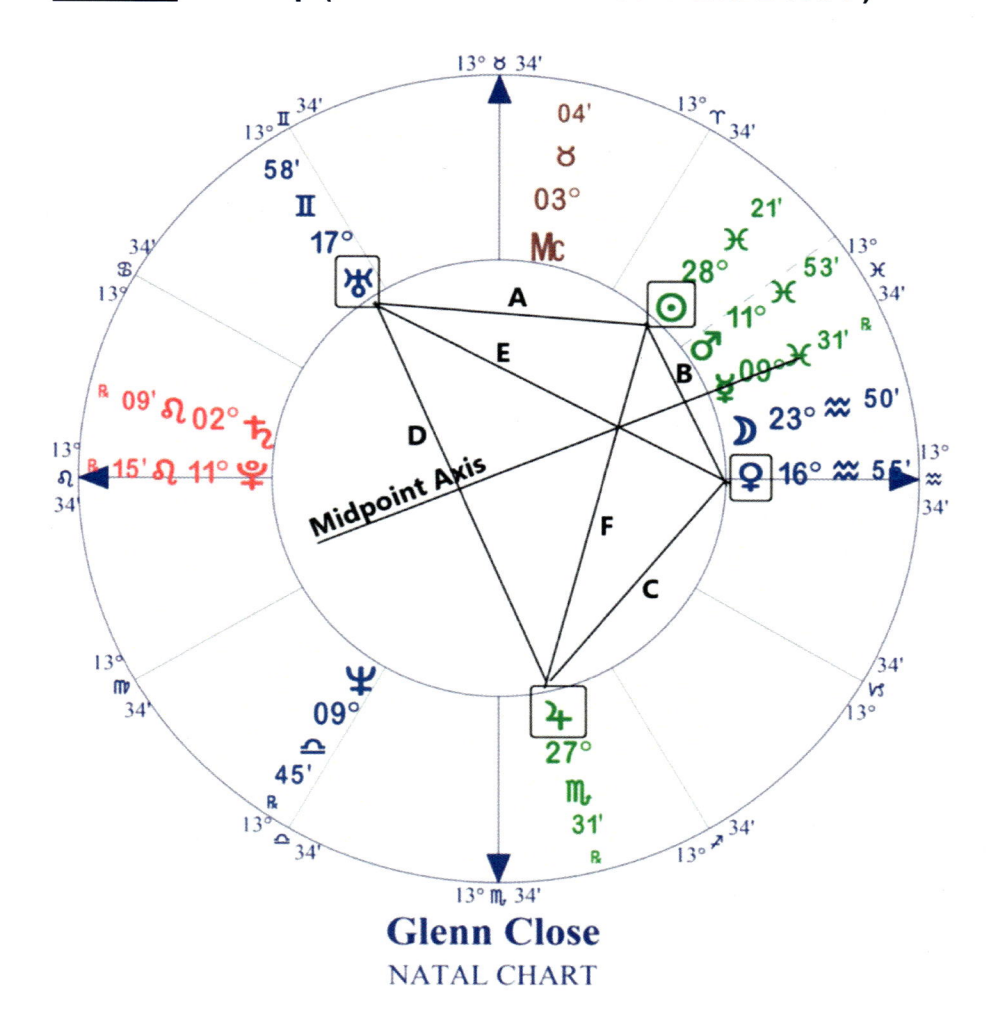

Glenn Close
NATAL CHART

Basic VA Chart Interpretation

To visually detect a possible isotrap in a chart, look for two lines of the same aspect that cross approximately at the same point. If the midpoints of the pairs of planets fall within orb, an isotrap will be present.

In **Figure 6**, the Trine aspect between Sun-Jupiter and the Trine aspect between Venus-Uranus increase the strength of the Isotrap **(Figure 5)**

Figure 6: Natal Chart Isotrap referenced in Figure 5

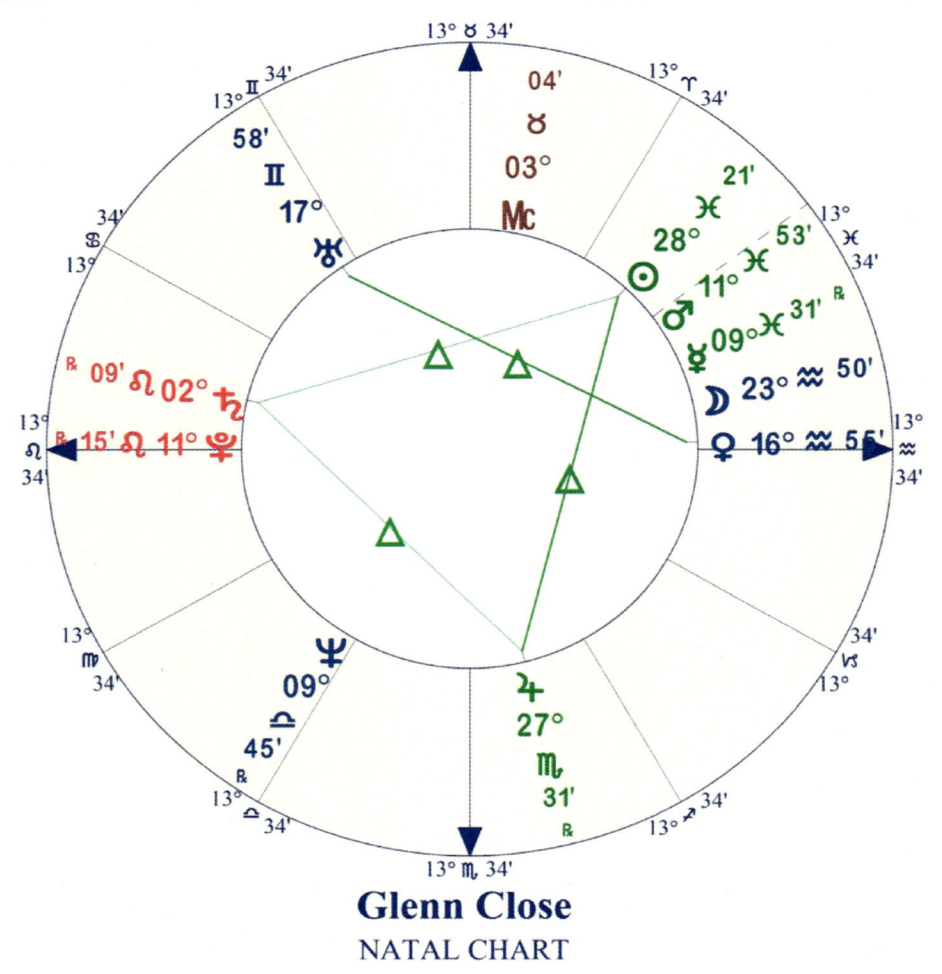

Glenn Close
NATAL CHART

Vibrational Astrology Study Guide Module One

If an isotrap is suspected or no visible isotraps are present, one of the two options below may be used to verify the presence of isotraps. (Remember: The planets involved in the isotrap may not be aspected.)

Option 1: In Sirius Astrology Software, the **Midpoints-to-Midpoints Report** allows one to quickly identify isotraps in a chart. Access the report as follows:
1. In Menu Bar, Select "Listing"
2. Click "Harmonic Patterns Listings"
3. Check "1=Harmonic Triangles, Quadrangles & Midpt-to-Midpt"
4. Click "OK"

The Midpoints-to-Midpoints Report is located at the bottom of the "Harmonic Patterns Listings Report #1", "Harmonic Triangles, Quadrangles & Midpt-to-Midpt" Report. **(Figure 7)**

The isotraps are divided into orb categories of <15', 15'-30', 30'-1°, and 1-3°. The orb for an isotrap is believed to be very small but this has to be researched. In the meantime, reading isotraps in the less than 30' categories is recommended. In **Figure 7**, the 15' Minute Orb category shows the strongest isotraps in the "Midpoints to Midpoints" Report in the chart of Glenn Close. Her 15' Minute Midpoint to Midpoint Alignment is starred (**) and references her isotrap in **Figures 5&6**.

Figure 7: "Midpoints to Midpoints" Report (Harmonic Patterns Listing #1)

Glenn Close
March 19, 1947
2:12 PM
Greenwich, Connecticut

MIDPOINTS TO MIDPOINTS
Midpoints conjunct/opposition Midpoints with 15 Minute Orb
Sun/Venus opposition Jupiter/Uranus. Orb: 0 deg 07 min
Mercury/Mars opposition Neptune/Pluto. Orb: 0 deg 12 min

Midpoints conjunct/opposition Midpoints with 15 to 30 Minute Orb
Sun/Moon conjunct Mercury/Mars. Orb: 0 deg 23 min

Midpoints conjunct/opposition Midpoints with 30 Minute to 1 Degree Orb
Sun/Moon opposition Neptune/Pluto. Orb: 0 deg 35 min
Moon/Jupiter opposition Saturn/Uranus. Orb: 0 deg 37 min

Midpoints conjunct/opposition Midpoints with 1 to 3 Degree Orb
Sun/Uranus conjunct Venus/Saturn. Orb: 1 deg 22 min
Moon/Mercury conjunct Venus/Mars. Orb: 2 deg 17 min
Moon/Saturn conjunct Venus/Pluto. Orb: 1 deg 05 min

Copyright © The Avalon School of Astrology, Inc. All Rights Reserved
All chart wheels and reports used in this module are created from Sirius 3.0 with permission from Cosmic Patterns Software

Option 2: 180° Midpoint Sort

Viewing the 180° Midpoint Sort, look for midpoint planet locations that are less than 1.5° apart. The closer the midpoints, the stronger the isotrap.

The location in the 180° sort can be visually identified by estimating the signs of the Midpoint Axis in the chart. In **Figure 5**, this would be Virgo and Pisces. Choosing the sign in the first six signs in the zodiac since we are using a 180-degree midpoint sort, estimating the degrees in 360° notation yields between 150-179° (Virgo degrees). In this case, it appears to be in early Virgo or near the 150-165° location. The actual midpoint is 157° as shown in **Figure 8**.

Figure 8: 180 Degree Midpoint Sort showing an Isotrap

Glenn Close
NATAL CHART Tropical/Equal

☉
♃–♄ 1°30'

☽

☿
♆–♇ 0°59'

♀

♂
☉–☽ 0°48'
♆–♇ 1°23'

♃
♂–♇ 0°57'

♄

♅
☽–♆ 1°11'

♆

♇

180 Degree Midpoint Sort:

♃/♇ 4°23'	♀/♄ 39°32'	♃ 57°31'	☉/♆ 94°03'	♄ 122°09'	♀/♂ 149°24'	☿/♂ 160°42'
♆ 9°45'	☽/♄ 43°00'	☉/♄ 60°15'	♀/♃ 97°13'	♄/♇ 126°42'	☽/☿ 151°41'	☉/☽ 161°05'
♀/♅ 17°27'	♀/♇ 44°05'	☉/♇ 64°48'	♄/♅ 100°04'	♇ 131°15'	☽/♂ 152°51'	♂ 161°53'
☽/♅ 20°54'	☽/♇ 47°32'	♀/♆ 73°20'	☽/♃ 100°41'	♅/♆ 133°52'	[illegible]	☉/☿ 168°56'
☿/♅ 28°45'	☿/♄ 50°50'	☽/♆ 76°47'	♅/♇ 104°37'	♀ 136°55'	☉/♀ 157°38'	☉/♂ 170°07'
♂/♅ 29°56'	♂/♄ 52°01'	♅ 77°58'	☿/♃ 108°31'	☽/♀ 140°22'	♃/♅ 157°45'	☉ 178°21'
♃/♆ 33°38'	☿/♇ 55°23'	☿/♆ 84°38'	♂/♃ 109°42'	☽ 143°50'	[illegible]	♃/♄ 179°50'
☉/♅ 38°10'	♂/♇ 56°34'	♂/♆ 85°49'	☉/♃ 117°56'	☿/♀ 148°13'	♆/♇ 160°30'	

Utilizing the 360° Midpoint Sort, locate the two areas that hold the two ends of the Midpoint Axis (Virgo and Pisces). Look for midpoints that are close enough to be within orb of a conjunction or opposition. In this case, Jupiter/Uranus @ 7°45' Virgo and Sun/Venus @ 7°38' Pisces meet the criteria. **(Figure 9)**

Figure 9: 360 Degree Midpoint Sort showing and Isotrap

Glenn Close
NATAL CHART Tropical/Equal

Midpoint Listing:

♀/♅ 17♈27	☽/♇ 17♉32	♄/♅ 10♋04	♆/♇ 10♍30	☿/♆ 24♐38	♀ 16♒55	☿ 9♓31
☽/♅ 20♈54	☿/♄ 20♉50	♅/♇ 14♋37	♃/♄ 29♍50	♂/♆ 25♐49	☽/♀ 20♒22	☿/♂ 10♓42
☿/♅ 28♈45	♂/♄ 22♉01	♄ 2♌09	♃/♇ 4♎23	☉/♆ 4♑03	☽ 23♒50	☉/☽ 11♓05
♂/♅ 29♈56	☿/♇ 25♉23	♄/♇ 6♌42	♆ 9♎45	♀/♃ 7♑13	☿/♀ 28♒13	♂ 11♓53
☉/♅ 8♉10	♂/♇ 26♉34	♇ 11♌15	♃/♆ 3♏38	☽/♃ 10♑41	♀/♂ 29♒24	☉/☿ 18♓56
♀/♄ 9♉32	☉/♄ 0♊15	♅/♆ 13♌52	♃ 27♏31	☿/♃ 18♑31	☽/☿ 1♓41	☉/♂ 20♓07
☽/♄ 13♉00	☉/♇ 4♊48	♄/♆ 5♍57	♀/♆ 13♐20	♂/♃ 19♑42	☽/♂ 2♓51	☉ 28♓21
♀/♇ 14♉05	♅ 17♊58	♃/♅ 7♍45	☽/♆ 16♐47	☉/♃ 27♑56	☉/♀ 7♓38	

Vibrational Astrology Study Guide Module One

A **Triple Isotrap** is composed of three midpoints within orb of being conjunct or opposite each other. Thus, six different planets are creating three midpoints that have all the midpoints within orb and no planets at the focal point. This results in 6 resonances, two from each isotrap. A Triple Isotrap is very powerful when the orbs are very small.

Note: Double Isotrap is a redundant term because an isotrap already has two midpoints that are aligned. Thus, a Double isotrap is the same as an isotrap.

A Triple Isotrap can be located in a chart by reviewing the Midpoints-to-Midpoints Report for duplicated planetary midpoints. Three stars have been inserted to more easily identify the three alignments that form the Triple Isotrap. **(Figure 10)** Following is a listing of the three alignments with the repeating midpoint structures highlighted.

> **Moon/Mercury** opposition **Jupiter/Neptune**. Orb: 0 deg 28 min
> **Moon/Mercury** conjunct Venus/Uranus. Orb: 0 deg 44 min
> Venus/Uranus opposition **Jupiter/Neptune**. Orb: 1 deg 12 min

Figure 10: Midpoint-to-Midpoints Report of Triple Isotrap
MIDPOINTS TO MIDPOINTS

Midpoints conjunct/opposition Midpoints with 15 to 30 Minute Orb

Moon/Venus conjunct Mars/Uranus. Orb: 0 deg 16 min
Moon/Pluto conjunct Mercury/Saturn. Orb: 0 deg 29 min
Mercury/Pluto conjunct Venus/Saturn. Orb: 0 deg 22 min
Moon/Mercury opposition Jupiter/Neptune. Orb: 0 deg 28 min

Midpoints conjunct/opposition Midpoints with 30 Minute to 1 Degree Orb

Moon/Mercury conjunct Venus/Uranus. Orb: 0 deg 44 min
Venus/Pluto conjunct Mars/Saturn. Orb: 0 deg 51 min
Mars/Neptune conjunct Uranus/Pluto. Orb: 1 deg 00 min
Mercury/Mars opposition Jupiter/Saturn. Orb: 0 deg 35 min

Midpoints conjunct/opposition Midpoints with 1 to 3 Degree Orb

Sun/Venus opposition Jupiter/Saturn. Orb: 2 deg 56 min
Sun/Mars opposition Jupiter/Pluto. Orb: 2 deg 05 min
Venus/Jupiter opposition Saturn/Neptune. Orb: 1 deg 47 min
Venus/Uranus opposition Jupiter/Neptune. Orb: 1 deg 12 min
Mars/Jupiter opposition Neptune/Pluto. Orb: 2 deg 38 min

A **Spreading Triple Isotrap** occurs if one of the three midpoints is slightly out of orb.

Basic VA Chart Interpretation

5. Midpoint Isotraps

A **Midpoint Isotrap,** shown in a midpoint tree, is a configuration of 5 different planets occurring when a planet is the focal planet of an isotrap. The midpoints in the Midpoint Isotrap can be any combination of conjunctions and oppositions. The greater the number of different planets involved in a midpoint pattern, the more significant the pattern. The tighter the midpoint patterns, the more dominant the combination will be. Its importance is increased by the presence of the midpoints and isotrap.

A Midpoint Isotrap contains four resonances due to its configuration. The midpoint planet resonates with each planetary pair yielding two resonances. In addition, there are two resonances within the isotrap itself. (**Figure 11**)

The midpoint with the smallest orb is tighter, therefore more influential. If the midpoint planet resonances are smaller, then their influence is greater. If the isotrap has tighter orbs than the midpoint planets, the isotrap resonances will have more influence. The pattern should be read accordingly, focusing on the strongest planetary resonance influences first.

Vibrational Astrology Study Guide Module One

A Midpoint Isotrap example is Sat opp Mer/Ven @ 0°02' and Sat opp Mars/Plu @ 0°22' shown in the midpoint tree (**Figure 11**). The Isotrap will appear as an isosceles trapezoid (isotrap) in the chart with a planet at the midpoint. The "red" lines in **Figure 11** show the Isotrap structure that is formed. (Resonances: Mar-Sat res Sat-Plu (Black); Mer-Sat res Ven-Sat (Green); Mer-Mar res Ven-Plu (Orange); Ven-Mar res Mer-Plu (Purple))

<u>**Figure 11**</u>: **Midpoint Isotrap (5 Planets, 4 Resonances)**

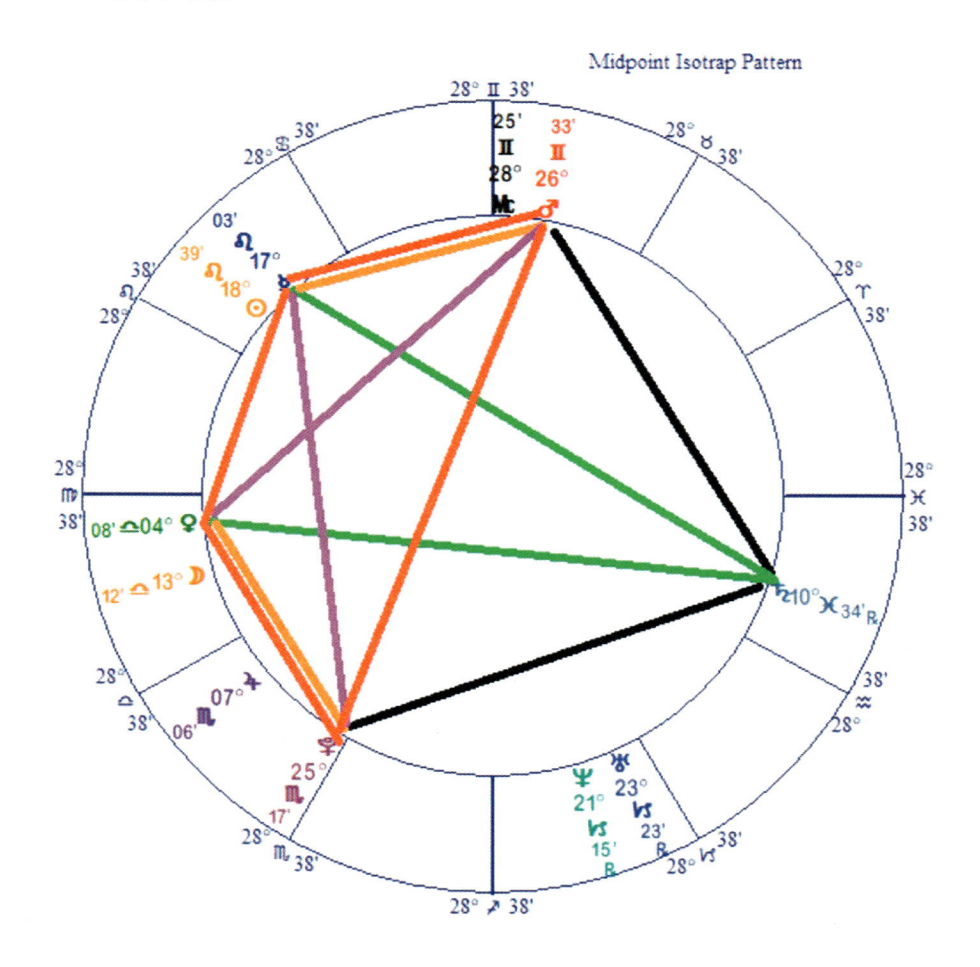

Basic VA Chart Interpretation

A **Triple Midpoint Isotrap** is composed of three midpoints conjunct or opposite each other that have a planet at the focal point within orb. No duplication of planets. **(Figure 12)** The Triple Midpoint Isotrap is a seven-planet configuration. With seven different planets, this yields three isotraps and nine resonances.

In **Figure 12**, the black lines show the Focal Planet and its relationship to each of the three pairs of surrounding planets. The red, green, and blue lines indicate the isotraps formed by the three planetary pairs having a common Focal Point. The Focal Planet's interaction with each of the three pairs yields three resonances. Each of the isotraps has two resonances. Therefore, the three isotraps contribute 6 resonances to the structure, totaling 9 (3+6) resonances in all.

Figure 12: Triple Midpoint Isotrap (7-Planets, 3 Isotraps, 9 Resonances)

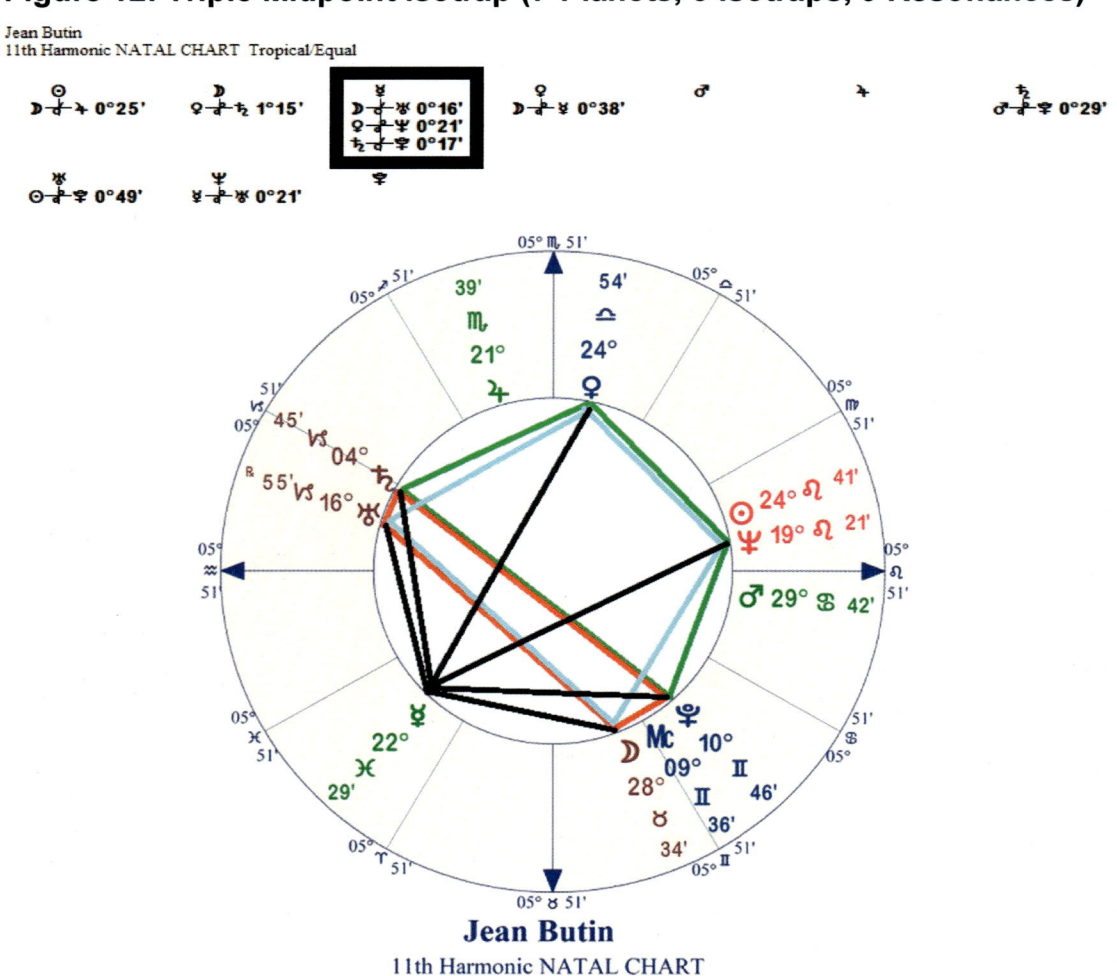

Resonance is not the only thing that determines the strength of a midpoint configuration, but it appears to be a very important one. Another important factor is whether all of the planets in the configuration are also strongly aspected to each other in some vibration.

The significance of resonances is not completely confirmed yet in data-driven research studies, but personal observations appear to support the idea that the number of resonances helps estimate the strength of a midpoint configuration, and this midpoint configuration is important.

The following chart of Midpoint Patterns and their related resonances applies only to configurations where no planets are duplicated in the structure. **(Figure 13)**

Figure 13: **Midpoint Patterns with # of Resonances** (No duplication of planets in the configurations)

Midpoint Patterns	# Planets	# Resonances
Quadruple Midpoint Isotrap	9	16
Triple Midpoint Isotrap	7	9
Midpoint Isotrap	5	4
Quadruple Isotrap	8	12
Triple Isotrap	6	6
Isotrap	4	2
Power Midpoint Structure	4	3
Midpoint Structure	3	1

Adding different planets to any configuration will increase that pattern's significance, and likely the number of resonances, making it more significant in the client's life.

In summary, a vibrational midpoint structure is very important when the orb is less than 0°30' or there are midpoint patterns less than 1° (Midpoint Isotrap, Isotrap). When a Midpoint Isotrap or Isotrap is aspected in the chart, it is much stronger than if it is unaspected. A 4-5+ planet midpoint pattern will be very significant!

Basic VA Chart Interpretation

D. How to Read an Astrology Chart Using VA

1. Confirm Birth Information and Source
Higher vibrations are very dependent on the birth time being within a few minutes of exact.

2. Natal Chart – ("HJJ" Chart (K=Big, Large Inner Area) in Sirius Astrology Software is recommended.)

Observe Ptolemaic aspects less than 1° and Non-Ptolemaic aspects (Semisextile, Semisquare, Sesquiquadrate) approximately 30' or less. If no conjunction or opposition aspects are present less than 1° for Ptolemaic or 0°30' for non-Ptolemaic aspects, expand the aspect orb to include aspects less than 1°30' and 1°00' respectively. The Quincunx and 1/16th aspects are treated separately.

VA focuses on the interpretation of three (3) or more planets creating energy patterns. In the natal chart, planets are tightly aspected when they have an orb less than 1° for Ptolemaic aspects or less than 0°30' for non-Ptolemaic aspects. **These orbs indicate that a particular aspect pair is an energy line strong enough for the person to feel it in other vibrations.** When two planets are tightly aspected, but they are not both aspecting a third planet, they are interpreted as a trait, rather than a behavior. The vibrations where these two planets are joined by a third planet give additional information needed to describe a behavior. In the natal chart, midpoint patterns with orbs less than 0°15' can be read directly as descriptions of the person's behaviors.

Note: If the Natal Chart contains strong conjunctions, it may be read as the 1-Vibration, especially if it has large conjunction patterns. It shows the extent to which the person is self-referenced and self-directed rather than other-referenced.

Vibrational Astrology Study Guide Module One

3. Midpoint Patterns

Review Midpoint Trees for Tight Midpoint Structures and Midpoint Isotraps and the "Midpoints to Midpoints" Report (Harmonic Patterns Listing #1) and/or the 180° or 360° Midpoint Sort for Isotraps.

Reminder: **Aspects create an obvious and straightforward effect. Midpoint Structures and Isotraps, when activated, are more subtle, refined, and sophisticated than aspect patterns.**

4. Harmonic Listing #8 (Figure 14)

In Sirius Astrology Software, **Harmonic Listing #8** Identifies strong Midpoint Structures and the Vibration(s) where the planets in a midpoint form a 3-planet conjunction. Access the report as follows:
  1. In Menu Bar, Select "Listing"
  2. Click "Harmonic Patterns Listings"
  3. Select "8=Direct Midpoint Structures and Harmonic 1-128"
  4. Click "OK"

What to look for:
- Midpoints with small orbs and their vibrations
- Vibrations that have small orbs
- Vibrations that are multiples of lower vibrations
- Repeating vibrations, especially less than 32

Basic VA Chart Interpretation

Figure 14: Direct Midpt Structures and Harmonic 1-128 (Harmonic Listing #8):

Billie Jean King
November 22, 1943   11:45 AM
Long Beach, California   33 N 46 01   118 W 11 18
Tropical Equal War Time observed
GMT: 18:45:00   Time Zone: 8 hours West

Sun	29 Sco 36	Mars	17 Gem 36	Neptune	3 Lib 42
Moon	0 Lib 44	Jupiter	26 Leo 21	Pluto	8 Leo 43
Mercury	6 Sag 34	Saturn	24 Gem 58	Asc.	27 Cap 14
Venus	13 Lib 04	Uranus	7 Gem 07	MC	16 Sco 24

Direct Midpoint Structures of Sun-Pluto within 2 deg orb and harmonic (1 to 128) with 16 degree orb in harmonic chart:

```
Ven Cnj Sun/Jup 0 deg 06 min, and 23rd (prime) Harmonic with orb= 15 deg 16 min
Ven Cnj Sun/Jup 0 deg 06 min, and 31st (prime) Harmonic with orb = 10 deg 43 min
Ven Cnj Sun/Jup 0 deg 06 min, and 54th (9x6)   Harmonic with orb = 7 deg 49 min
Ven Cnj Sun/Jup 0 deg 06 min, and 85th (17x5)  Harmonic with orb = 11 deg 49 min
Ven Cnj Sun/Jup 0 deg 06 min, and 108th(9x12)  Harmonic with orb = 15 deg 38 min
Nep Cnj Sun/Plu 0 deg 28 min, and 13th (prime) Harmonic with orb = 6 deg 42 min
Nep Cnj Sun/Plu 0 deg 28 min, and 26th (13x2)  Harmonic with orb = 13 deg 23 min
Plu Cnj Moo/Mar 0 deg 27 min, and  7th (prime) Harmonic with orb = 4 deg 08 min
Plu Cnj Moo/Mar 0 deg 27 min, and 14th (7x2)   Harmonic with orb = 8 deg 17 min
Plu Cnj Moo/Mar 0 deg 27 min, and 21st (7x3)   Harmonic with orb = 12 deg 25 min
Plu Cnj Ven/Ura 1 deg 23 min, and 123rd(41x3)  Harmonic with orb = 15 deg 51 min
```

In this case, make note of the 9th, 17th, 23rd, and 31st Vibrations related to the Ven cnj Sun/Jup @ 0°06', 13th Vibration related to Nep cnj Sun/Plu @ 0°28' and the 7th Vibration related to Plu cnj Moo/Mar @ 0°27'.

5. Harmonic Listing #1 (Figure 15)

Harmonic Listing #1 will identify 4-Planet conjunctions in Vibrations less than 360°. (**Figure 15**)
Access the report in Sirius Astrology Software as follows:
1. In Menu Bar, Select "Listing"
2. Click "Harmonic Patterns Listings"
3. Select "1=Harmonic Triangles, Quadrangles, and Midpt-to-Midpt"
4. Click "OK"
5. Section: "4-Planet Conjunctions in Harmonic Charts"

What to look for:
- Orb totals less than 8 degrees. If an orb is 8 degrees or less, it is very strong, and the planets will be capitalized.
- Repetition of a vibration on several lines of the listing

A 4-planet Conjunction in orb is very important, even in higher harmonics (16-360).

Figure 15: "4-Planet Conjunctions in Harmonic Charts" (Harmonic Listing #1)

Astrological Data for

Billie Jean King
November 22, 1943
11:45 AM
Long Beach, California

33 N 46 01   118 W 11 18   Tropical EQUAL
War Time observed   GMT: 18:45:00
Time Zone: 8 hours West

Harmonics 1 to 360, 16 Degree Orb in Harmonic Chart
(Duplicates are removed, i.e. not listed if orbs small and therefore conjunct in a lower harmonic or first harmonic)

4-PLANET CONJUNCTIONS IN HARMONIC CHARTS:

*20: Mercury-Saturn-Venus-Uranus, 11 deg (Mercury-8-Saturn-2-Venus-1-Uranus) 5x4
21: Pluto-Mars-Jupiter-Moon, 12 deg (Pluto-7-Mars-4-Jupiter-2-Moon)   7x3
41: Uranus-Pluto-Jupiter-Saturn, 11 deg (Uranus-5-Pluto-3-Jupiter-3-Saturn)   41
49: Pluto-Mercury-Mars-Saturn, 16 deg (Pluto-15-Mercury-1-Mars-1-Saturn)   7x7
49: Mercury-Mars-Saturn-Moon, 14 deg (Mercury-1-Mars-1-Saturn-13-Moon)   7x7
135: Sun-Saturn-Jupiter-Neptune, 14 deg (Sun-4-Saturn-7-Jupiter-2-Neptune)   9x5x3 or 45x3
220: Sun-Mars-Jupiter-Moon, 11 deg (Sun-2-Mars-4-Jupiter-6-Moon)   11x5x4 or 55x4

Basic VA Chart Interpretation

240: Venus-Sun-Mars-Uranus, 12 deg (Venus-5-Sun-2-Mars-5-Uranus)   5x3x16 or 15x16
241: Uranus-Mars-Jupiter-Neptune, 14 deg (Uranus-5-Mars-7-Jupiter-1-Neptune)   241
241: Mars-Jupiter-Neptune-Moon, 15 deg (Mars-7-Jupiter-1-Neptune-7-Moon)   241
263: PLUTO-SUN-MOON-URANUS, *** 1 DEG *** (Pluto-1-Sun-0-Moon-0-Uranus)   263
263: PLUTO-SUN-MOON-VENUS, *** 6 DEG *** (Pluto-1-Sun-0-Moon-5-Venus) 263
263: Pluto-Sun-Moon-Saturn, 12 deg (Pluto-1-Sun-0-Moon-11-Saturn)   263
263: PLUTO-SUN-URANUS-VENUS, *** 6 DEG *** (Pluto-1-Sun-0-Uranus-5-Venus)   263

Reviewing Billie Jean King's data from Harmonic Listings #1 & #8, one notices that the 7th vibration shows up several times. (**Figures 14 & 15**)

6. Vibrations for Beginning Astrological Screening

Following are the recommended vibrations for beginning astrological screening in interpretations.

    8-Vibration
    5-Vibration
    7-Vibration
    9-Vibration
    11-Vibration
    13-Vibration

Note: 8-Vibration shows what you feel you have to do; 5, 7, & 9-Vibrations are essential to the person's development. The development of at least one of the three latter vibrations opens the door to developing higher vibrations

Vibrations higher than 13 will be addressed in Module 2, Chapter 6. Note that vibrations 17 and 19 are also fundamental and basic vibrations, although beginning students may stop at 13-Vibration.

Everyone has strong and weak vibrations. A weak vibration only means that the person is not as focused in the particular area represented by that vibration.

Vibrational Astrology Study Guide Module One

7. Aspect Pattern Review

Two planet combinations in the natal chart would be felt as an internal trait and not necessarily a behavior pattern. One does not read two planet patterns in vibrational charts.

Review the vibrations for energy circuits of 3 or more planets that adhere to the Aspect Rules for Vibrational Charts (Chapter 3, Section F). In vibrations where an energy circuit is formed, determine that the energy circuit is "active" in that vibration by verifying that at least one fractional denominator is evenly divisible by the vibration number.

A planetary connection of three or more planets is required for the energy to flow in a circuit. View the planets as processes. The chart shows how the energy wants or needs to flow, not how it will manifest. A strong aspect indicates a strong need in the person but does not guarantee that they are conscious of that need. The goal is to get the energy to flow constructively and to increase the person's consciousness of and connection with their ways of operating to enhance their well-being and effectiveness.

Referring to Billie Jean King's information presented earlier, we were alerted to the potential significance of the 7-Vibration from the Harmonic Listing Reports #1 **(Figure 15)** & **#8 (Figure 14)**. We know that Pluto, Moon, and Mars are connected in a midpoint less than 0°30' adding importance to these planets in the 7-Vibration. The addition of Venus' attraction to beauty and sense of proportion (square) to Moon-Mars-Pluto would add to the beauty of her performance. The smooth support (Trine) of Jupiter would enable her to improve, growing and expanding her capabilities as well as augmenting the basic drive of Moon-Mars-Pluto. The Jupiter trine Pluto increases the compulsive push toward success in the 7-Vibe emphasizing the disciplined inner focus of 7 and enhancing her ability to be successful. (**Figure 16, 7-Vibration right**)

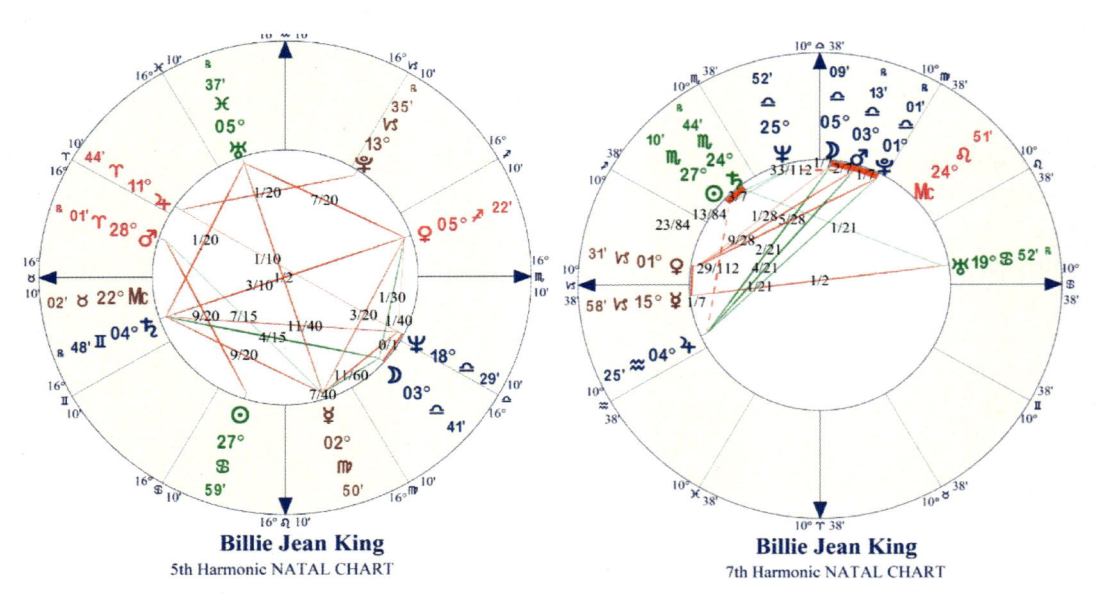

Basic VA Chart Interpretation

Figure 16: **5th and 7th Vibrations - Most Significant Vibrations in Billie Jean King's Chart**

Billie Jean King
5th Harmonic NATAL CHART

Billie Jean King
7th Harmonic NATAL CHART

With the review of the vibrational charts 13 and less, we see Mercury, Venus, Saturn and Uranus connected in a Grand Cross in the 5-Vibration (also seen in Harmonic Listing #1(starred)). This configuration tells us of her dynamic ability to "play" (5-Vibe), the drive to achieve (Square aspects), the use of her high intelligence (Mercury-Venus), analytical ability (Mercury-Saturn),+ and quick thinking (Mercury-Uranus) to become one of the greatest women tennis players of all time. (**Figure 16, 5-Vibration left**)

Aspects containing the Inner Planets, Sun, Moon, Mercury, Venus, Mars, generate behaviors that the person identifies with, feeling as if they are the source of those thought processes, feelings, attractions, motivations, etc. An aspect circuit consisting solely of planets beyond Mars (Jupiter, Saturn, Uranus, Neptune, Pluto) results in an experience that feels like it is coming from outside. These impersonal aspect patterns can still be strong determiners of behavior. If there are one or more inner planets involved with the outer planets, the behavior will be experienced as personal.

When reading planets and aspects, remember that planets serve the vibration. They never overpower the vibration.

In summary, in each vibration, interpret the vibration, adapt the planetary aspect patterns and midpoint structures to the vibration, and then interpret them together.

110

Copyright © The Avalon School of Astrology, Inc. All Rights Reserved
All chart wheels and reports used in this module are created from Sirius 3.0 with permission from Cosmic Patterns Software.

Vibrational Astrology Study Guide Module One

E. Summary: Basic VA Chart Interpretation

The Natal Chart is the only real chart. Vibrational charts are derived from the natal chart. The denominator of the natal aspect fraction in the natal chart identifies the vibration where the two planets will be conjunct. I.e., a square or 1/4th aspect would be conjunct in the 4-Vibration.

The **orbs** in all charts must be proportional to maintain consistency between the natal and vibrational charts. Proportional orbs used in VA are shown below.

Proportional Orbs in Vibrational Astrology

Aspect	Orb	Calculation
Conjunction (0°)	16°	(16/1)
Opposition (180°)	8°	(16/2)
Square (90°)	4°	(16/4)
Trine (120°)	5°20'	(16/3)
Sextile (60°)	2°40'	(16/6)
Semisquare (45°)	2°00'	(16/8)
Sesquiquadrate (135°)	2°00'	(16/8)
Semisextile (30°)	1°20'	(16/12)
Quincunx (150°)	1°20'	(16/12)
1/16th Aspect (22.5°)	1°00'	(16/16)

Midpoints:

A **Midpoint** is a point halfway between two planets.

A **Focal Point** is a point that is conjunct or opposite the midpoint of two other planets.

A **Focal Planet** is a planet located at the focal point, conjunct or opposite the midpoint of two planets.

A **Slash (/)** always indicates the midpoint.

"=" or "AT" indicates a planet is conjunct or opposite the midpoint of two other planets.

Basic VA Chart Interpretation

A **Parentheses "()"** indicates planets that are working together. If no aspect is shown, then a conjunction is assumed.

A **Midpoint Structure** is formed when one planet (focal planet) is conjunct or opposite the midpoint of two other planets. The terms, **Near Midpoint** (conjunction) and **Far Midpoint** (opposition), are used to differentiate between the two forms of Midpoint Structures.

A **Midpoint Axis or Symmetry Axis** is the line of symmetry between the conjunction (near) midpoint and opposition (far) midpoint of the midpoint structure.

A **Tight Midpoint Structure** indicates a midpoint structure with a very small orb (0-20 minutes).

A **Strong Midpoint Structure** is synonymous with a Tight Midpoint Structure, but its meaning is not as clear. The astrology of a "strong midpoint structure" may take into account additional considerations, such as the focal planet is almost exactly on an angular house cusp or some other planetary, nodal, or asteroid relationship.

A **Weak Midpoint Structure** occurs when the orb of the midpoint structure is relatively large and not part of a large midpoint tree. In VA, a weak midpoint structure would have an orb greater than 1°15' or 1°20'.

Surrounding Planets reference the two planets surrounding the focal planet in a Midpoint Structure.

A **Midpoint Tree** is a diagram that shows a focal planet with one or more midpoint structures.

A **Resonance** occurs when the angular distances between pairs of planets match or are within orb. In resonances, the energetic stimulation of one of the pairs of planets will also stimulate the second pair of planets.

Vibrational Astrology Study Guide Module One

Resonances must be stimulated to vibrate. When they are stimulated, the resonance provides a delicacy, a sensitivity, an ability to work with fine details. This enables the midpoint pattern to express itself with refinement and finesse that is not available in an aspect circuit.

There are several ways to activate a resonance:
1. Within the vibration, a planetary circuit (or aspected pair of planets) involving the planets in the midpoint will be an ongoing activation of that midpoint.
2. A conjunction of the three planets in a related vibration.
3. Another person's chart can activate the midpoint.
4. Transits and Progressions can temporarily activate the midpoint
5. Once the midpoint is activated the person may well continue to use it, providing mental stimulation of their own to resonate with it.

A **Midpoint Resonance** is a single midpoint structure composed of either a near or far midpoint having one resonance. A **Midpoint Tree** has varying resonances.

A **Power Midpoint Structure** is a midpoint structure where one of the planets forms a conjunction with another planet and both are within orb in the Midpoint Structure. The Power Midpoint Structure contains 3 resonances.

Direct Midpoint Structure is synonymous with **Midpoint Structure**. Sirius Software occasionally uses the term Direct Midpoint Structure to specify the type of report for astrologers unfamiliar with VA.

Indirect Midpoint Structures refer to planets making aspects other than conjunction or opposition to the midpoint of two other planets. These midpoint aspects are **NOT** used in VA.

How to interpret a midpoint structure: Focus on the planet in the middle and connect to the energy of the two planets that produce the midpoint. Simply combine the planetary meanings. With multiple midpoints, combine in decreasing order of strength, strongest first.

Basic VA Chart Interpretation

Isotraps:

An **Isotrap** is a shortened term for an Isosceles Trapezoid. There are three ways to describe an isotrap.
- It is two pairs of planets that are separated by nearly the same angular distance. No planet is positioned at the midpoint.
- It is a four (4) planet pattern in which a midpoint is conjunct or opposite another midpoint.
- Another term for conjunct or opposite the same midpoint is a **Midpoint-to-Midpoint Alignment or Midpoint Alignment**.
- Note: All four planets must be different.

The terms, **Alignment and Aligned**, are used to indicate planets that are in conjunction or opposition with one another or on an axis.

A **Midpoint Isotrap** is a configuration of 5 different planets occurring when a planet is the focal planet of two midpoint structures having any combination of conjunctions and oppositions.

Midpoint Patterns with # of Resonances (No duplication of planets in the configurations)

Midpoint Patterns	# Planets	# Resonances
Quadruple Midpoint Isotrap	9	16
Triple Midpoint Isotrap	7	9
Midpoint Isotrap	5	4
Quadruple Isotrap	8	12
Triple Isotrap	6	6
Isotrap	4	2
Power Midpoint Structure	4	3
Midpoint Structure	3	1

Vibrational Astrology Study Guide Module One

Reading the Astrological Chart using VA:

1. Confirm birth information and source.
2. Natal Chart: Note Ptolemaic Aspects <1° and minor aspects <30'.
3. Review Midpoint Trees for Tight Midpoint Structures and Midpoint Isotraps in addition to the "Midpoints to Midpoints" Report (Harmonic Patterns Listing #1) and/or the 180° or 360° Midpoint Sort for Isotraps. Midpoint Orbs may be evaluated as follows:

    <0°15'   = Extremely Strong
    >0°15'-<0°30' = With an inner planet is Very Strong
    >0°30'- <1°   = Solid, definitely there but needs to be reinforced
                           by other planets
    >1°- <1°30'   = There, but not necessarily conspicuous

4. Review Harmonic Patterns Listing #8 (Identifies Vibrations up to 128 connected to Midpoints)
Look for: Midpoints with small orbs and their vibrations
        Vibrations that have small orbs
        Vibrations that are multiples of lower vibrations
        Repeating vibrations, especially less than 3

5. Review Harmonic Patterns Listing #1 (Identifies 4-Planet conjunctions in Vibrations up to 360)
Look for: Orb totals less than 8 degrees. If an orb is 8 degrees or less, it
        is very strong and the planets will be capitalized
        Repetition of a vibration on several lines of the listing

6. Review planetary patterns and midpoint structures in Vibrations: 8,5,7,9,11,13.
Everyone has strong and weak vibrations. A weak vibration only means that the person is not as focused in the particular area represented by that vibration.

7. Aspect Pattern Review: Two planet combinations in the natal chart can be seen as traits and not necessarily behaviors. A planetary connection of three or more planets is required for the energy to flow. Verify the energy circuit is connected to the vibration and therefore "active" in that vibration. View the planets as energy processes. The chart shows how the energy wants or needs to flow, not how it will manifest.

Basic VA Chart Interpretation

Review: Rules for Reading Aspect Patterns:
Aspect Line Colors:
> Solid Red Lines: Conjunctions, Oppositions, Squares, Semisquares, Sesquiquadrates
> Dashed Red Lines: 1/16th Aspects
> Solid Green Lines: Trines, Sextiles, and Semisextiles
> Solid Brown Lines: Quincunxes

a. All planets (3 or more) connected by "Solid Red" aspects (Conjunction, Opposition, Square, Semisquare, Sesquiquadrate) may be read

b. All planets (3 or more) connected by "Solid Green" (Trine, Sextile, Semisextile) aspects may be read

c. Combining Red and Green Only: "Red" conjunction and opposition aspects combine with "Green" aspects when in a pattern (3 or more planets)

e. The 1/16, 3/16, 5/16, and 7/16ths aspects are forming energy circuits, however, those circuits can be better understood if one doubles the vibration.

f. The Quincunx is NOT included in energy circuits.

In each vibration, interpret the vibration, adapt the planetary aspect patterns and midpoint structures to the vibration, and then interpret them together. (Remember: Planets serve the vibration; they never overpower the vibration.)

Note: The term "Vibration" is synonymous with the term "Harmonic" used in report titles.

Vibrational Astrology Study Guide Module One

F. Books & Videos

Books

Berry, Linda & Cochrane, David, *Vibrational Astrology, Interpreting Aspects,* Gainesville: Cosmic Patterns Software, inc., 2016. (Order through http://www.Lulu.com)

Cochrane, David, *Vibrational Astrology, the Essentials,* Gainesville, Florida: Cosmic Patterns Software, Inc, 2021

Videos

Astrology Tutorial Videos by David Cochrane
Https://www.astrologydc.com

Introduction to VA Course, Part 1
The Power of Exact Direct Midpoint Structures
Interpreting Midpoint Structures with Vibrational Astrology
Midpoint Structure: Their Use in Cosmobiology and Vibrational Astrology
VA Fundamentals in Detail, Part 1,2,3,4,5,6,7,8
VA Fundamentals in Detail, Part 1 Addendum
Interpretation of Astrology Birth Charts of Rock 'n Roll Musicians

Introduction to VA Course, Part 2
How to Interpret a Birth Chart Using Vibrational Astrology: The Birth Chart of Marilyn Monroe
Natal Chart Interpretation with Vibrational Astrology: An Introduction

Aspects and Vibrational Charts
What a Harmonic Chart Is and How to Interpret It, Parts 1,2,3,4,5,6,7

Midpoints and Isotraps
Interpreting Midpoint Structures with Vibrational Astrology
The Power of Exact Direct Midpoint Structures
Midpoint Structures: Their Use in Cosmobiology and Vibrational Astrology
Harmonic Charts, Part 7: Octaves, Orbs, and Midpoints

Notes

Vibrational Astrology Study Guide Module One

SUMMARY COMPENDIUM

CHAPTER 2: VA Planet Descriptions & 2-Planet Combinations

Note: The parentheses in red indicate a "catchphrase", a distinctive trait or characteristic present.

Planets

Sun – (Clear & present reality)
The Sun connects us to the current moment and regulates what we are conscious of at any given time.

Moon – (Past into the present)
The Moon brings the past into the present, regulating what elements of the past we are aware of.

Mercury – (Makes mental connections)
Mercury makes mental connections and communicates; sees relationships and associations, noticing and comparing similarities and differences.

Venus – (Attraction to beauty)
Venus regulates the magnetic power of attraction to beauty.

Mars - (A force to achieve, drive)
Mars is the dynamic force needed to achieve, the drive to reach a goal.

Jupiter – (Grows & expands)
Jupiter is the energy force that grows and expands. Without Jupiter, there is no growth.

Saturn – (Removes all that is superficial)
Saturn is the energy force that removes all that is superficial to discover the essence, the foundations, the essential core.

Uranus – (Acts spontaneously)
Uranus is the energy force that acts in the current moment without regard for the past or future.

Neptune – (Attraction to dreams, visions, ideals)
Neptune is the force of attraction to dreams, visions, ideals.

Pluto - (Compulsive & obsessive energy)
Pluto is energy from the deep past that expresses itself forcefully as compulsiveness or even obsession.

Summary Compendium

Planet Combinations

Sun

Sun-Moon – *(Brings past into present view)*
Appreciates how the past is the basis or foundation of the present bringing the hidden or shadowed into the light of the present

Sun-Mer – *(Speaks, writes clearly)*
Brings clear and present thought and communication

Sun-Ven – *(Appreciation of simplistic beauty)*
A clear and present beauty

Sun-Mars – *(Loves activity in work & play)*
A clear and present force to achieve, a drive to do something tangible, something real

Sun-Jup – *(Desires growth)*
A clear and present ongoing growth and expansion

Sun-Sat – *(Focus on essentials)*
A clear and present desire to get rid of everything that is not essential

Sun-Ura – *(Spontaneous, quick to laugh & respond)*
Attunes to the waves and cycles of the moment expressing them as a clear and present spontaneity

Sun-Nep – *(Child-like optimism)*
Brings a clear and present sense of attraction to the wonder and magic of dreams, visions, and ideals

Sun-Plu – *(Life of passion & mission)*
Makes daily life compulsive and obsessive.

Copyright © The Avalon School of Astrology, Inc. All Rights Reserved
All chart wheels and reports used in this module are created from Sirius 3.0 with permission from Cosmic Patterns Software.

Vibrational Astrology Study Guide Module One

Moon

Moon-Mer – *(Thoughts of past)*
Thinking about the past and how the past influences the present
Moon-Ven – *(Attracted to soul, depth, long heritage)*
Attraction to the beauty of the past
Moon-Mars – *(Wants to achieve, accomplish)*
Enjoys the feeling of accomplishment and is always seeking to improve its skills
Moon-Jup – *(Warm, friendly, welcoming)*
Has expansive moods and enjoys an open atmosphere
Moon-Sat – *(Sincere, quiet, introverted)*
Has a need for isolation that quiets the emotions enabling one to perceive deep essential long-lasting truths
Moon-Ura – *(Emotionally Impulsive)*
Needs to feel free and unrestricted by expectations and consequences
Moon-Nep – *(Emotionally sensitive)*
Sensitive to the atmosphere and mood
Moon-Plu – *(Compulsive eruptions of feeling)*
Powerful concentrations of past feelings erupt forcefully into the present

Mercury

Mer-Ven – *(Verbal intelligence, Literary ability)*
Attraction to the power of a beautiful idea
Mer-Mar – *(Needs to learn & understand)*
Energizes, stimulates, and acts on mental processes
Mer-Jup – *(Open-minded; Sees big picture)*
Connects ideas together forming an expansive pattern
Mer-Sat – *(Analytical)*
Analyzing to eliminate the superfluous and find the essence
Mer-Ura – *(Clever, Quick thinker)*
Connects ideas in the present moment
Mer-Nep – *(See magic and wonder in life)*
Attraction to fascinating, idealistic, visionary thoughts
Mer-Plu – *(Opinionated)*
Connects ideas obsessively or compulsively

Summary Compendium

Venus

Ven-Mars – *(Needs tangible, sensual life experiences)*
Accomplishing based on an attraction to the beauty that is alive, visceral, and real

Ven-Jup – *(Outgoing & Friendly)*
Attraction to the beauty that is expansive

Ven-Sat – *(Sincere & Honest)*
Attraction to the beauty that gets to the essential core

Ven-Ura – *(Rhythm, Dance, Music)*
Attraction to the beauty that is rhythmic, exciting, and spontaneous

Ven-Nep – *(Magic & Romance)*
An inspired, dreamy attraction to beauty

Ven-Plu – *(Passionate, powerful, irresistible internal force)*
Compulsive, obsessive attraction to beauty

Mars

Mars-Jup – *(Wants to achieve big things)*
A force of expansive accomplishment

Mars-Sat – *(Does the "dirty work")*
A force to accomplish the essential things that need to be done

Mars-Ura – *(Ability to respond quickly)*
A sudden burst of energy to achieve a goal

Mar-Nep – *(Sees magic in everyday life)*
The force to accomplish one's dream

Mar-Plu - *(Driven by passion)*
A force of obsessive, compulsive achievement

Jupiter

Jup-Sat – *(Planning & strategy)*
Essential, regulated growth

Jup-Ura – *(Excited, enthusiastic, "Good Luck" Aspect)*
Growth and expansion that is concentrated and electrified by the waves of the moment

Jup-Nep – *(Gives Inspiration)*
Seeking bigger, more expansive fantasies and dreams

Jup-Plu – *(Has a sense of destiny & mission)*
A compulsive need to become larger and grander

Saturn

Sat-Ura – *(Brings clarity now)*
Uranus modifies and electrifies Saturn's focus making it impatient to get to the essence right now

Sat-Nep – *(Uncovers deeper meaning of life)*
Removes superficial glitter and glamour to get to honest, sincere, fundamental, long-lasting ideas, ideals, and visions

Sat-Plu – *(Severe, Ascetic)*
Obsessive about removing everything to get to the essence

Uranus

Ura-Nep – *(Sensitive, May be visionary)*
Amazing, out of this world visionary experiences occurring through attunement to the waves of the moment

Ura-Plu – *(Needs freedom)*
A compulsive need to be operating in the moment

Neptune

Nep-Plu – *(Mission & purpose)*
An obsessive need to follow a dream or vision

Notes

Vibrational Astrology Study Guide Module One

CHAPTER 3: Aspects & Orbs

Ptolemaic aspects:
Conjunctions are adjacent to each other (0°) (Orb: 16°)
Oppositions are opposite each other (180°) (½) (Orb 8°)
Trine aspects have the same sign **Element (Fire, Earth, Air, Water)** (120°) (⅓) (Orb: 5°20') (4 signs apart)
Square aspects have the same sign **Mode (Cardinal, Fixed, Mutable)** (90°) (¼) (Orb: 4°) (3 signs apart)
Sextile aspects are in signs that are **two (2) signs apart** (60°) (⅙) (Orb: 2°40')

Elements: Fire Signs (Aries, Leo, Sagittarius)
  Earth Signs (Taurus, Virgo, Capricorn)
  Air Signs (Gemini, Libra, Aquarius)
  Water Signs (Cancer, Scorpio, Pisces)

Modes: Cardinal Signs (Aries, Cancer, Libra and Capricorn)
  Fixed Signs (Taurus, Leo, Scorpio, Aquarius)
  Mutable Signs (Gemini, Virgo, Sagittarius, Pisces)

Ptolemaic aspects are identified by the aspect glyph in the Natal Chart. In the Vibration Chart, the aspects may be identified by the element, mode, signs, line color, degrees of separation, and/or the glyph in the Aspect Grid.

Non-Ptolemaic Aspects:
Semisquare (45°) (⅛) (Orb: 2°)
Sesquiquadrate (135°) (⅜) (Orb: 2°)
Semisextile (30°) (1/12) (Orb: 1°20')
Quincunx (150°) (5/12) (Orb: 1°20')
1/16th Aspect (22.5°) (1/16) (Orb: 1°)

Non-Ptolemaic aspects are identified by the aspect glyph or a dashed aspect line in the Natal Chart. In the Vibrational Chart, the aspects may be identified by line color, a solid or dashed aspect line, degrees of separation, and/or glyph in the Aspect Grid.

Summary Compendium

Aspect interpretations:

Conjunction (0°) - Conjunctions involve planets that are adjacent to one another and get their meaning from the planets that aspect them. Combine their meanings with the vibration they occupy. They show the basic energy expressions and driving force in a person's life.

Opposition (180°) (½) - Oppositions create a polarity between the planets yielding an interest in sharing or conflicting with others

Square (90°) (1/4th) - Squares are a need to take action, providing the motivation and drive to do something, make changes, make progress or achieve a goal.

Trine (120°) (1/3rd) - Trines show unrestricted energy flow that is easy and tends to be smooth.

Sextile (60°) (1/6th) - Sextiles want to share in an easy, free-flowing manner.

Semisquare (45°) (1/8th) - Semisquares are what one has to do. They define one's mode of operation when one takes action.

Sesquiquadrate (135°) (3/8th) - Sesquiquadrates are similar to Semisquares except that they are more easily and naturally expressed and somewhat less stressful.

Semisextile (30°) (1/12th) - Semisextiles balance action and flow. They are a strongly ingrained quality.

Quincunx (150°) (5/12th) – Quincunxes represent energies that need to be developed. The vibration is the main descriptor of the growth needed with the two planets further refining the growth process. There is a strong motivation for these energies to grow into a useful mature behavior. If this growth process is unsuccessful then this trait will not be available in this vibration.

1/16, 3/16, 5/16, 7/16th Aspects (22.5°) (1/16th) - The 1/16th aspects indicate an action that originates in conscious internal processing that is not obvious to others. The 1/16th aspects are forming energy circuits; however, those circuits can be better understood by doubling the vibration.

Interpretation involves combining the meaning of the vibration with the meaning of the planets and aspects in the vibrational circuit.

Copyright © The Avalon School of Astrology, Inc. All Rights Reserved
All chart wheels and reports used in this module are created from Sirius 3.0 with permission from Cosmic Patterns Software.

Vibrational Astrology Study Guide Module One

Proportional Orbs:
An **orb** is the allowable difference between the planetary arc and the exact aspect.

Proportional orbs are required for the natal and vibrational aspects to parallel one another.

An aspect's strength is determined by the exactitude of the orb. The smaller the orb, the stronger the aspect, the larger the orb the weaker the aspect.

Proportional Orbs in VA:

Aspect	Max Orb
Ptolemaic Aspects	
Conjunction (0°)	16°
Opposition (180°)	8°
Square (90°)	4°
Trine (120°)	5°20'
Sextile (60°)	2°40'
Non-Ptolemaic Aspects	
SemiSquare (45°)	2°00'
Sesquiquadrate (135°)	2°00
Semi-Sextile (30°)	1°20'
Quincunx (150°)	1°20'
1/16th Aspect (22.5°)	1°00

Aspect Rules:
Aspects in Vibrational Astrology require a third planet to complete an energetic circuit in each aspect configuration. Three or more planets connected through aspects require the application of the following rules to be read as energy circuits.

Settings for Aspect Lines:
Solid Red Lines: Conjunction, Opposition, Square, Semisquare, Sesquiquadrate
Dashed Red Lines: 1/16th aspects
Solid Green Lines: Trine, Sextile, and Semisextile
Solid Brown lines: Quincunx

Using the above criteria, the following rules for reading aspect energy flow apply:
   a. All planets (3 or more) connected by "Solid Red" aspect lines may be read.
   b. All planets (3 or more) connected by "Solid Green" aspect lines may be read.
   c. Combining Red and Green aspects: "Red" conjunction or opposition aspects combine with "Green" aspects when in a pattern of 3 or more planets

Active & Inactive Vibrational Circuits:

All aspect circuits of three planets or more in a vibration must have at least one fraction denominator on one of the aspect lines that is evenly divisible by the vibration to connect the circuit into that vibration and therefore be active in that vibration. If no aspect line denominators are evenly divisible by the vibration to connect the circuit into the vibration, that circuit is not active and cannot be read in that vibration.

Aspect Patterns in VA:

In VA, only five aspect patterns are identified by name: **Grand Trine, T-Square, Yod, Grand Cross,** and the **Kite**. All other patterns are described by the aspects composing the circuit.

Grand Trine: Three planets connected by Trine aspects (approximately 120° within orb) in the same Element (Fire, Earth, Air, Water Signs)

T-Square: Three planets, two defined by an Opposition aspect with the third Squaring the two oppositional planets

Yod: Three planets connected by two Quincunxes and a Sextile

Grand Cross: Four planets all located approximately Square (90° apart within orb), the Opposition planets creating a cross

Kite: Four planet aspect pattern composed of a Grand Trine with one planet opposite one of the points of the Grand Trine (all within orb) (Looks like a kite!)

"Power" aspect structure: The term, **"Power"**, preceding an aspect structure (or midpoint structure) describes a conjunction that adds an additional planet to the structure, thereby increasing the structure's significance in the life of the person.

"Double Power" aspect structure: The term, "Double Power", indicates the presence of two sets of conjunctions on different single planetary positions in a planetary structure.

"**Spreading**" indicates aspects that are slightly or only minutes out of orb. These aspect circuits are weaker than when all aspects are in orb.

Aspect Grids:

The **Aspect Grid** provides aspect information at a glance. In addition to the standard aspects normally shown, the VA astrologer often includes the Quintile (5-Vibe), Septile (7-Vibe), Novile (9-Vibe), 11-Vibe, and 13-Vibe for quick reference.

Notes

Vibrational Astrology Study Guide Module One

CHAPTER 4: VA Vibrations: Energy Processes (EP) & Behaviors (1-13)

A summarization of the energy processes and behavioral symptoms of vibrations one through thirteen are listed below. With each prime number in the vibrational sequence, a new behavioral characteristic(s) is introduced. **Vibrations of <u>Prime Numbers</u> are highlighted and underlined below.**

<u>The Natal Chart – A combination of all the potential vibrations of the person, the life's patterns in all their complexity.</u>

Keywords or "catchphrases", listed below, are provided in parentheses in red as a reminder or trigger for the basic meanings or behaviors of the first 13 vibrations.

<u>1-Vibration</u> - (Self)
Energy: Using the internal sense of what is essential to the person to direct the life
Note: The 1-Vibration is read as a vibrational chart only when it contains significant conjunction patterns relative to the other vibrational charts.
Behavior: Self-directed behavior is a fundamental characteristic of the person

<u>2-Vibration</u> – (Polarity, Sharing)
Energy: Polarized interaction/exchange with something outside yourself
Behavior: How we interact with each other, how we share and/or oppose others.

<u>3-Vibration</u> - (Smooth & Harmonious)
Energy: Free, unrestricted, smooth flow of energy
Behavior: Represents an easy flow between the planets involved

4-Vibration - (Motivation & Drive)
Energy: A need rising from within that shapes what one is driven to do
Behavior: Motivation & drive to have an impact and to change circumstances

<u>5-Vibration</u> - (Playfulness & Creativity)
Energy: An organic exploration and interaction that is nonlinear and outwardly directed
Behavior: Natural process of exploration; often experienced as joyful play and satisfying creative discovery

Summary Compendium

6-Vibration – (Harmonious Interaction with Others)
Energy: The free flow of interactive energy
Behavior: Wants to share with others in a free-flowing manner

7-Vibration – (Quiet, Meditative, Introverted)
Energy: Quieting, internalizing, deepening one's energy, and formulating internal understandings
Behavior: Quiet, deep, introverted, has intense concentration and self-discipline; forms own internal world, may utilize abstract or symbolic thinking

8-Vibration - (Action)
Energy: Action that makes a difference
Behavior: Engages in a concrete action that manifests results

9-Vibration – (Integration & Bonding; Healing & Soothing)
Energy: The process of integration and bonding with the environment
Behavior: Deals with areas of integration, and connectedness to one's eclectic group or circle; Has a healing, soothing quality that can bring wholeness and a feeling of contentment

Note: 5-, 7-, and 9-Vibrations are essential for psychological health. The development of at least one of these opens the door to developing higher vibrations.

10-Vibration - (Play and Creative Expression with Others)
Energy: Organic exploration and interaction that is shared with others
Behavior: Engages in shared experiences of interaction, organic exploration, play, and creativity

11-Vibration – (Progressive, Restless, Hungry for Change)
Energy: Restless, dissatisfied, reaching out for something more or different, desires change
Behavior: Restless and dissatisfied with the present circumstances; tends to be progressive; tends to be easily bored and needs stimulation

12-Vibration – (Combines Challenging & Dynamic with Free-flowing)
    Energy: Seeks to balance the push outward of motivation and drive, with receptivity that is coming in so that there is an easy flow between yourself and others
    Behavior: A gentle, smooth flowing receptivity is operating in union with an outward movement that is conveying one's motivations and drives. The motivation and drive must be expressed in a way that generates a smooth harmonious interaction with others.

13-Vibration – (Moves Beyond Average or Mediocre)
    Energy: Going deep within, seeking to uncover one's distinct essence and make it the new operating center of life
    Behavior: Has a drive to move beyond the average and mediocre; An inherent need to discover a special or exceptional essence that is deeply felt and a willingness to work hard to find and connect with this essence.

Summary of "catchphrases" for Vibrations 1-13:
1-Vibration – Self
2-Vibration – Polarity, Sharing
3-Vibration – Smooth & Harmonious
4-Vibration – Motivation & Drive
5-Vibration – Playfulness & Creativity
6-Vibration – Harmonious Interaction with Others
7-Vibration – Quiet, Meditative, Introverted
8-Vibration – Action
9-Vibration – Integration & Bonding; Healing & Soothing
10-Vibration – Play & Creative Expression with Others
11-Vibration – Progressive, Restless Hungry for Change
12-Vibration – Combines Challenging & Dynamic with Free-flowing
13-Vibration – Moves Beyond Average or Mediocre

Notes

CHAPTER 5: Basic VA Chart Interpretation

The Natal Chart is the only real chart. Vibrational charts are derived from the natal chart. The denominator of the aspect fraction in the natal chart identifies the vibration where the two planets will be conjunct. I.e., a square or 1/4th aspect would be conjunct in the 4-Vibration.

The **orbs** in all charts must be proportional to maintain consistency between the natal and vibrational charts. Proportional orbs used in VA are shown below.

Proportional Orbs in Vibrational Astrology

Aspect	Max Orb
Ptolemaic Aspects	
Conjunction (0°)	16°
Opposition (180°)	8°
Square (90°)	4°
Trine (120°)	5°20'
Sextile (60°)	2°40'
Non-Ptolemaic Aspects	
Semisextile (30°)	1°20'
Quincunx (150°)	1°20'
Semisquare (45°)	2°00'
Sesquiquadrate (135°)	2°00'
1/16th Aspect (22.5°)	1°00'

Midpoints:

A **Midpoint** is a point halfway between two planets.

A **Focal Point** is a point that is conjunct or opposite the midpoint of two other planets.

A **Focal Planet** is the planet located at the focal point, conjunct or opposite the midpoint of two planets.

A **Slash (/)** always indicates the midpoint.

"=" or "AT" indicates a planet is conjunct or opposite the midpoint of two other planets.

Summary Compendium

A **Parentheses "()"** indicates planets that are working together. If no aspect is shown, then a conjunction is assumed.

A **Midpoint Structure** is formed when one planet (focal planet) is conjunct or opposite the midpoint of two other planets. The terms, **Near Midpoint** (conjunction) and **Far Midpoint** (opposition), are used to differentiate between the two forms of Midpoint Structures.

A **Midpoint Axis or Symmetry Axis** is the line of symmetry between the conjunction (near) midpoint and opposition (far) midpoint of the midpoint structure.

A **Tight Midpoint Structure** indicates a midpoint structure with a very small orb (0-20 minutes).

A **Strong Midpoint Structure** is synonymous with a Tight Midpoint Structure, but its meaning is not as clear. The astrology of a "strong midpoint structure" may take into account additional considerations, such as the focal planet is almost exactly on an angular house cusp or some other planetary, nodal, or asteroid relationship.

A **Weak Midpoint Structure** occurs when the orb of the midpoint structure is relatively large and not part of a large midpoint tree. In VA, a weak midpoint structure would have an orb greater than 1°15' or 1°20'.

Surrounding Planets is a term used to describe the two planets surrounding the focal planet in a Midpoint Structure.

A **Midpoint Tree** is a diagram that shows a focal planet with one or more midpoint structures.

Vibrational Astrology Study Guide Module One

A **Resonance** occurs when the angular distances between pairs of planets match or are within orb. In resonances, the energetic stimulation of one of the pairs of planets will also stimulate the second pair of planets.

Resonances must be stimulated to vibrate. When they are stimulated, the resonance provides a delicacy, a sensitivity, an ability to work with fine details. This enables the midpoint pattern to express itself with refinement and finesse that is not available in an aspect circuit.

There are several ways to activate a resonance:
1. Within the vibration, a planetary circuit (or aspected pair of planets) involving the planets in the midpoint will be an ongoing activation of that midpoint.
2. A conjunction of the three planets in a related vibration.
3. Another person's chart can activate the midpoint.
4. Transits and Progressions can temporarily activate the midpoint
5. Once the midpoint is activated the person may well continue to use it, providing mental stimulation of their own to resonate it.

A **Midpoint Resonance** is a single midpoint structure composed of either a near or far midpoint having one resonance. A **Midpoint Tree** has varying resonances.

A **Power Midpoint Structure** is a midpoint structure where one of the planets forms a conjunction with another planet and both are within orb in the Midpoint Structure. The Power Midpoint Structure contains 3 resonances.

Direct Midpoint Structure is synonymous with **Midpoint Structure.** Sirius Software occasionally uses the term Direct Midpoint Structure to specify the type of report for astrologers unfamiliar with VA.

Indirect Midpoint Structures refer to planets making aspects other than conjunction or opposition to the midpoint of two other planets. These midpoint aspects are **NOT** used in VA.

How to interpret a midpoint structure: Focus on the planet in the middle and connect to the energy of the two planets that produce the midpoint. Simply combine the planetary meanings. With multiple midpoints, combine in decreasing order of strength, strongest first.

Isotraps:

An **Isotrap** is a short-term for an Isosceles Trapezoid. There are three ways to describe an isotrap.
- It is two pairs of planets that are separated by nearly the same angular distance. No planet is positioned at the midpoint.
- It is a four (4) planet pattern in which a midpoint is conjunct or opposite another midpoint.
- Another term for conjunct or opposite the same midpoint is a **Midpoint-to-Midpoint Alignment or Midpoint Alignment**.
- Note: All four planets must be different planets.

The terms, **Alignment and Aligned**, are used to indicate planets that are in conjunction or opposition with one another or on an axis.

A **Midpoint Isotrap** is a configuration of 5 different planets occurring when a planet is the focal planet of two midpoint structures having any combination of conjunctions and oppositions.

Midpoint Patterns with # of Resonances (No duplication of planets in the configurations)

Midpoint Patterns	# Planets	# Resonances
Quadruple Midpoint Isotrap	9	16
Triple Midpoint Isotrap	7	9
Midpoint Isotrap	5	4
Quadruple Isotrap	8	12
Triple Isotrap	6	6
Isotrap	4	2
Power Midpoint Structure	4	3
Midpoint Structure	3	1

Vibrational Astrology Study Guide Module One

Reading the Astrological Chart using VA:

1. Confirm birth information and source.
2. Natal Chart: Note Ptolemaic Aspects <1° and minor aspects <30'.
3. Review Midpoint Trees for Tight Midpoint Structures and Midpoint Isotraps in addition to the "Midpoints to Midpoints" Report (Harmonic Patterns Listing #1) and/or the 180° or 360° Midpoint Sort for Isotraps. Midpoint Orbs may be evaluated as follows:

    <0°15'   = Extremely Strong
    >0°15'-<0°30' = With an inner planet is Very Strong
    >0°30'- <1°   = Solid, definitely there but needs to be reinforced
                           by other planets
    >1°- <1°30'   = There, but not necessarily conspicuous

4. Review Harmonic Patterns Listing #8 (Identifies Vibrations up to 128 connected to Midpoints)
Look for: Midpoints with small orbs and their vibrations
       Vibrations that have small orbs
       Vibrations that are multiples of lower vibrations
       Repeating vibrations, especially less than 3

5. Review Harmonic Patterns Listing #1 (Identifies 4-Planet conjunctions in Vibrations up to 360)
Look for: Orb totals less than 8 degrees. If an orb is 8 degrees or less, it
       is very strong and the planets will be capitalized
       Repetition of a vibration on several lines of the listing

6. Review planetary patterns and midpoint structures in Vibrations: 8,5,7,9,11,13.
Everyone has strong and weak vibrations. A weak vibration only means that the person is not as focused in the particular area represented by that vibration.

7. Aspect Pattern Review: Two planet combinations in the natal chart can be seen as traits and not necessarily behaviors. A planetary connection of three or more planets is required for the energy to flow. Verify the energy circuit is connected to the vibration and therefore "active" in that vibration. View the planets as energy processes. The chart shows how the energy wants or needs to flow, not how it will manifest.

Summary Compendium

Review: Rules for Reading Aspect Patterns:

Aspect Line Colors:
- Solid Red Lines: Conjunctions, Oppositions, Squares, Semisquares, Sesquiquadrates
- Dashed Red Lines: 1/16th Aspects
- Solid Green Lines: Trines, Sextiles, and Semisextiles
- Solid Brown Lines: Quincunxes

a. All planets (3 or more) connected by "Solid Red" aspects (Conjunction, Opposition, Square, Semisquare, Sesquiquadrate) may be read

b. All planets (3 or more) connected by "Solid Green" (Trine, Sextile, Semisextile) aspects may be read

c. Combining Red and Green Only: "Red" conjunction and opposition aspects combine with "Green" aspects when in a pattern (3 or more planets)

e. The 1/16, 3/16, 5/16, and 7/16ths aspects are forming energy circuits, however, those circuits can be better understood if one doubles the vibration.

f. The Quincunx is NOT included in energy circuits.

In summary, in each vibration, interpret the vibration, adapt the planetary aspect patterns and midpoint structures to the vibration, and then interpret them together.
(Remember: Planets serve the vibration; they never overpower the vibration.)

Note: The term "Vibration" is synonymous with the term "Harmonic" used in report titles.

Notes

Notes

Vibrational Astrology Study Guide Module One

Glossary of Terms

"=" or "AT": Indicates a planet is conjunct or opposite the midpoint of two other planets

Alignment or Aligned: Sometimes used to indicate planets that are conjunct or opposite; planets on an axis in conjunction or opposition

Arc: The distance between two planets or points in an astrological chart. This is usually expressed in degrees, minutes, seconds, or decimal degrees.

Aspect: An aspect is an arc or number of degrees of the circle that can also be represented as a fraction of the circle. It is related to the distance between any two planets or points within an astrological chart. An aspect does not have to be exact. See orb.

Aspect Grid: The aspect grid provides information on the planetary aspects, either abbreviated or by symbol, with or without the degree of separation.

Aspects, Non-Ptolemaic: Aspects added by other astrologers after Claudius Ptolemy wrote "Tetrabiblios".
    Semisextile = 30° or 1/12th of the circle - The Semisextile balances action and flow. It is a strongly ingrained quality.
    Semisquare = 45° or 1/8th of the circle - The Semisquare is similar to a square, but it <u>has</u> to take an action. It defines one's mode of operation when one takes action.
    Sesquiquadrate = 135° or 3/8th of the circle - The Sesquiquadrate is similar to the semisquare. It is somewhat less stressful and more easily expressed.
    Quincunx = 150° or 5/12th of the circle - The Quincunx represents energy that needs to be developed. The vibration is the main descriptor of the growth needed with the two planets further refining the growth process. There is a strong motivation for the energy to develop into a useful mature trait. If this growth process is unsuccessful, this trait will not be available in this vibration. The Quincunx is not included in energy circuits.
    1/16th Aspect = 22.5° or 1/16, 3/16, 5/16, 7/16th of the circle - The 1/16th Aspects indicate an action that originates in conscious internal processing that is not obvious to others. The 1/16th Aspects are forming energy circuits however, those circuits can be better understood if one doubles the vibration.

Glossary of Terms

Aspects, Ptolemaic: Basic five astrological aspects originally identified by Greek astrologer, Claudius Ptolemy (100-170 CE), in his book, "Tetrabiblios".

> **Conjunction (0°)** - A Conjunction consists of two adjacent planets that acquire their meaning from the other planets that aspect them. Combine the meaning of the planets with the vibration they occupy.
> **Opposition = 180° or 1/2 of the circle** - An Opposition creates a polarity between the planets with an interest in sharing or conflicting with others.
> **Square = 90° or 1/4th of the circle** - Squares create an inner drive to take an action to achieve or make a change.
> **Trine = 120° or 1/3rd of the circle** - The Trine is an easy flow of energy that tends to be smooth.
> **Sextile = 60° or 1/6th of the circle** - Sextiles want to share in an easy, free-flowing manner.

Behavior: A distinctive way that one acts or conducts oneself either internally or in various types of external interaction

Base Vibration: The foundation vibration of a family of vibrations.

Characteristic: A distinctive way of operating

Denominator: The number below the line in a common fraction. (Ex. ⅕: 5 is the denominator)

Direct Midpoint Structure: Identical to the term, **Midpoint Structure**, in Vibrational Astrology (VA) and therefore is rarely used in VA. In Cosmobiology and other types of astrology that use additional aspects of planets to midpoints, a Direct Midpoint Structure refers to Midpoint Structures in which the aspect is a conjunction or opposition only. In Sirius Software, some report titles use the term, Direct Midpoint Structure, to differentiate the report from those used in other areas of astrology.

Family (of Vibrations): A series of vibrations that originates from a base vibration (Ex. 10, 15, 20, etc. are members of the 5 family of vibrations.). A Family of vibrations is formed by multiplying the base vibration (5 in the example) by all the integers: 5x1, 5x2, 5x3, 5x4, etc.

Focal Planet: The planet located at the focal point, conjunct or opposite the midpoint of two other planets

Focal Point: The point that is conjunct or opposite the midpoint of two other planets

Vibrational Astrology Study Guide Module One

Grand Cross: Four planets, all located approximately Square or 90° apart (within orb); i.e., the oppositional planets creating a cross

Grand Trine: Three planets connected by Trine aspects or approximately 120° (within orb) and in the same element (Fire, Earth, Air, Water Signs)

Harmonic: See Vibration

Harmonic Chart: See Vibrational Chart.

Indirect Midpoint Structure: References planets making aspects other than conjunction or opposition to the midpoint of two other planets. These midpoint relationships are **NOT** used in VA.

Isotrap: A four (4) planet pattern in which a midpoint is conjunct or opposite another midpoint. Another way of describing an isotrap is two pairs of planets that are separated by nearly the same angular distance. No planet is positioned at the midpoint location. The sides and diagonals of the isotrap are nearly equal in length and create two resonances. Isotrap is an abbreviation for Isosceles Trapezoid. May be described as a Midpoint-to-Midpoint Alignment. All 4 planets must be different.

Kite: A Grand Trine with one planet opposite one of the points of the Grand Trine, all within orb (Looks like a kite!)

Line of Symmetry: A line connecting the Near and Far Midpoints in a Midpoint Structure (Also called a Symmetry Axis or Midpoint axis)

Midpoint: The point halfway between two planets; This term may be used to reference the "near" or "far" midpoint.

Midpoint, Far: The point "opposite" the midpoint

Midpoint, Near: The point "conjunct" or at the same location as the midpoint

Midpoint Axis: A line of symmetry between two planets. (Also called Symmetry Axis or Line of Symmetry))

Midpoint Isotrap: A five (5) planet pattern having two planetary pairs that share the same midpoint with a planet at the focal midpoint. This pattern has four resonances: two resonances from the two midpoint structures and two resonances from the isotrap.

Glossary of Terms

Midpoint Structure: A three (3) planet pattern formed when one planet is **conjunct or opposite** the midpoint of two other planets (One resonance). (Example: Mercury opp Jupiter/Saturn)

Midpoint-to-Midpoint Alignment or Midpoint Alignment: A midpoint is conjunct or opposite another midpoint. The alignment of the planets creates an Isotrap or Isosceles trapezoid.

Midpoint Tree: When two or more midpoints have the same focal planet.

Numerator: The number above the line in a common fraction. (Ex. 2/5: 2 is the numerator).

Octave (Vibrational): The doubling of a vibration; Ex: next octave of the 5-Vibration is the 10-Vibration.

Orb: An orb is the allowable difference between the planetary arc and the exact aspect.

Orbs, Proportional: The conjunction orb (16') is the foundation used in calculating proportional orbs. The proportional orb of an aspect is the conjunction orb divided by the vibration number of the aspect. For the aspect in one vibrational chart to parallel the aspects in another vibrational chart, the orbs must be proportional.

Parentheses "(AND)": Indicates planets that are working together [Example: (Sun opp Mercury) = Moon/Mars] If no aspect is shown, then a conjunction is assumed: (Sun Mercury) = Moon/Mars.

Power: A term used to indicate an additional planet or planets is conjunct and within orb of the other planets within a larger aspect or midpoint structure. (Example: Power Grand Trine, Power Isotrap)

Prime Vibration: First-order or basic fundamental vibration

Quadruple Isotrap: Four (4) Midpoints within orb of being conjunct or opposite each other. No planets duplicated and no planet at the Midpoint.

Quadruple Midpoint Isotrap: Four (4) Midpoints within orb of being conjunct or opposite each other with a planet located at the focal point.

Quintuple Isotrap: Five (5) Midpoints within orb of being conjunct or opposite each other. No planets duplicated and no planet at the Midpoint.

Resonance (between planetary pairs): Resonance occurs when the angular distances between two pairs of planets match or are within orb. In resonances, the energetic stimulation of one of the pairs of planets also stimulates a second pair of planets.

Slash(/): Indicates the Midpoint of two planets. In other systems of astrology, the slash may be used loosely to mean any combination of planets. In VA, "/" always means Midpoint.

Spreading Aspect or Midpoint Pattern: When an aspected or midpoint planet or planets is slightly (only minutes) out of orb. Whenever at least one of the elements of a planetary configuration is out of orb, the planetary configuration is "spreading". It is weaker than an aspected or midpoint pattern within orb.

Spreading Triple Isotrap: If one of the 3 midpoint alignments is slightly out of orb of being conjunct or opposite each other. No planet at the midpoint.

Spreading Triple Midpoint Isotrap: Seven (7) planet midpoint pattern having three planetary pairs that share the same midpoint with a planet at the focal point. This pattern has 9 resonances: 3 from the three midpoint structures and 6 resonances from the three isotraps.

Strength, Aspect: How close the aspect orb is to exact; closer aspects have smaller orbs and are stronger.

Strength, Vibrational: The strength of a vibration is based on an evaluation of various interactions between the planets in each vibration. There can be different criteria for determining the comparative strength of different vibrations depending on the aspects and midpoint structures.

Strong Midpoint Structure: Both **Strong Midpoint Structure** and **Tight Midpoint Structure** are synonyms, but the Strong Midpoint Structure is not as clear in its meaning. There may be additional considerations for why a midpoint structure is strong, such as the astrologer taking into account that the focal planet is almost exactly on an angular house cusp or some other consideration.

Surrounding Planets: A term used to describe the two planets surrounding the focal planet in a Midpoint Structure

Symmetry Axis: A line of symmetry between two planets. (Also referred to as Midpoint Axis or Line of Symmetry)

T-Square: Three planets, two defined by an opposition aspect with the third squaring the two oppositional planets

Glossary of Terms

Tight Aspect: An aspect with a very small orb. (Example: In a vibrational chart in VA, a conjunction with an orb less than 3 degrees or a square less than 1 degree would be a tight aspect.)

Tight Midpoint Structure: Applies specifically to a midpoint structure with a very small orb, such as less than 15-20 minutes

Trait: A tendency that may color one's behaviors but is not as sharp, distinctive, and well-defined as a behavior. Traits are shown (1) by two planets that are in aspect to each other but do not form a circuit or (2) if a pattern is weak, then it tends to generate a tendency or trait.

Triple Isotrap: Three (3) Midpoints within orb of being conjunct or opposite each other. No planets duplicated and no planet at the Midpoint.

Vibration: The number by which a base chart is multiplied to create a vibrational chart. "Harmonic" is an equivalent term in Vibrational Astrology.

Vibrational Chart: A vibrational chart is an expansion of a base chart created by multiplying each planet and the Ascendant by the number of the vibration being constructed with each position converted to 360° notation.

Vibration Number: The vibration number of an aspect is the denominator of the fraction representing that aspect. It indicates the vibration where the two planets will be conjunct.

Weak Aspect or Midpoint Structure: When the orb of an aspect or midpoint structure is relatively large; In VA, a **Weak Midpoint Structure** would have an orb greater than 1°15' or 1°20'.

Yod: A three planet aspect consisting of two quincunxes and a sextile.

INDEX

1/16th Aspects, *45, 48, 50, 62, 63, 64, 104, 115, 125, 126, 127, 140, 143*
4-Planet Conjunction, *107*
Active circuit, *vii, 39, 52, 53, 65, 109, 128*
Active resonance, *3*
Addey, John, *2*
Aligned, *94, 113, 138, 143*
Alignment, *94, 113, 138, 143, 146*
Arc, *143*
Ascendent, *85*
Aspect, *vii, viii, 3, 34, 39, 47, 48, 50, 63, 64, 83, 84, 109, 115, 123, 126, 127, 139, 140, 143, 147, 148*
Aspect circuit, *10, 52, 54, 90, 110, 112, 137*
Aspect glyphs, *39, 88*
Aspect Grid, *vii, 39, 44, 61, 62, 66, 125, 129, 143*
Aspect Patterns, *vii, 39, 54, 65, 115, 128, 140*
Berry, Linda, *iv, 4, 6, 36, 66, 80, 116*
Catch phrases, *77, 79, 131, 133*
Charge, *4*
Cochrane, David, *iii, iv, 2, 6, 36, 66, 80, 85, 116*
Conjunction, *3, 40, 47, 50, 57, 58, 63, 64, 70, 84, 85, 115, 126, 127, 140, 144*
Cornelius, Geoffrey, *4*
Dean, Geoffrey, *4*
Denominator, *48, 49, 52, 53, 65, 83, 109, 111, 128, 135, 144, 148*
Dimension Reduction, *4*
Direct Midpoint, *93, 113, 137, 144*
Double Isotrap, *99*
Double Power, *59, 65, 128*
Ebertin, Reinhold, *2, 85*
Element,, *54*
Element, Air, *41, 54, 62, 65, 125, 128, 145*
Element, Earth, *41, 54, 62, 65, 125, 128, 145*
Element, Fire, *41, 54, 62, 65, 125, 128, 145*
Element, Water, *41, 62, 65, 125, 128, 145*
Elements, *39, 41, 42, 54, 62, 65, 125, 128*
Extreme Case Sampling, *2, 6, 11*
Family, *144*
Fink, David, *4*
Focal Planet, *88, 92, 102, 111, 135, 144*
Focal Point, *88, 102, 111, 135, 144*
Grand Cross, *54, 56, 65, 110, 128, 144*

Grand Trine, *54, 57, 58, 59, 65, 71, 128, 145*
Harmonic Listing #1, *viii, 83, 107, 110*
Harmonic Listing #8, *viii, 83, 105, 106*
Hellenistic astrology, *1*
Inactive circuit, *vii, 39, 52, 53, 65, 128*
Indirect Midpoint Structures, *93*
Isosceles Trapezoid, *94, 113, 138, 145*
Isotrap, *94, 95, 96, 98, 99, 100, 101, 102, 103, 113, 114, 138, 145, 146, 147, 148*
Kepler Astrology Software, *6*
Kepler, Johannes, *1*
Keywords, *77, 131*
Kite, *54, 57, 65, 128, 145*
Leo, Alan, *2*
Line of Symmetry, *88, 145, 147*
Mass, *4*
Midheaven, *85*
Midpoint, *viii, 83, 85, 86, 87, 88, 89, 90, 94, 97, 99, 100, 101, 102, 103, 111, 112, 113, 114, 135, 136, 137, 138, 145, 146, 147, 148*
Midpoint Alignment, *94, 97, 113, 138, 145, 146*
Midpoint Axis, *88, 94, 98, 112, 136, 145, 147*
Midpoint Listings, *85*
Midpoint Orbs, *viii, 83, 87, 114, 139*
Midpoint Settings, *viii, 83, 85*
Midpoint Sort, *98, 105, 114, 139*
Midpoint Structures, *85*
Midpoint Structures, *87, 88, 90, 91, 105, 106, 112, 113, 114, 116, 136, 137, 139, 144*
Midpoint Trees, *85, 92, 105, 114, 139*
Midpoint, Far, *88, 90, 112, 136, 145*
Midpoint, Near, *88, 112, 136, 145*
Midpoints-to-Midpoints Report, *97, 99*
Mode, Cardinal, *41, 62, 125*
Mode, Fixed, *41, 62, 125*
Mode, Mutable, *41, 62, 125*
Modes, *39, 41, 42, 62, 125*
Music of the Spheres, *1, 6*
New Moon chart, *85*
Non-Ptolemaic aspects, *39, 44, 62, 83, 104, 125*
Novile, *61, 66, 74, 129*
Numerator, *48, 83, 146*
Opposition, *3, 40, 47, 50, 55, 56, 63, 64, 65, 70, 84, 85, 115, 126, 127, 128, 140, 144*

Glossary of Terms

Orb, *39, 40, 49, 54, 56, 57, 60, 64, 65, 69, 70, 85, 87, 88, 89, 90, 92, 94, 96, 99, 100, 102, 103, 104, 106, 107, 112, 113, 114, 127, 128, 136, 137, 139, 143, 144, 145, 146, 147, 148*
Parentheses, *88, 112, 135, 146*
Pisano periods, *4*
Power aspect structure, *57, 65*
Power Grand Trine, *146*
Power Kite, *57*
Power Midpoint Structure, *92, 113, 137*
Prime number, *4, 69, 70, 71, 72, 75, 76, 77, 131*
Prime vibration, *69*
Progressions, *90, 113, 137*
Proportional orbs, *40, 49, 64, 84, 111, 127, 135, 146*
Ptolemaic aspects, *1, 39, 40, 43, 44, 62, 83, 104, 125*
Ptolemy, Claudius, *1, 6, 143, 144*
Pythagoras, *1*
Quincunx, *44, 46, 47, 50, 62, 63, 64, 75, 84, 104, 115, 125, 126, 127, 140, 143*
Quintile, *61, 66, 72, 83, 129*
Res, *90, 92, 95, 101*
Resonance, *90, 94, 103, 112, 113, 137, 146*
Semisextile, *3, 44, 47, 50, 62, 63, 64, 75, 84, 115, 125, 126, 127, 140, 143*
Semisquare, *3, 44, 47, 50, 52, 62, 63, 64, 84, 115, 125, 126, 127, 140, 143*
Septile, *61, 66, 73, 129*

Sesquiquadrate, *3, 44, 46, 47, 50, 52, 62, 63, 64, 84, 115, 125, 126, 127, 140, 143*
Sextile, *3, 40, 41, 42, 46, 47, 50, 55, 62, 63, 64, 65, 72, 84, 115, 125, 126, 127, 128, 140, 144*
Signs, *v, 39, 41, 42, 62, 65, 125, 128, 145*
Sirius, *ii, 3, 50, 61, 69, 93, 97, 104, 105, 107, 113, 137, 144*
Sirius Astrology Software, *6, 39, 50, 85, 97, 104, 105, 107*
Slash, *88, 111, 135, 147*
Space, *4*
Spin, *4*
Spreading, *60, 65, 99, 128, 147*
Square, *3, 40, 41, 42, 47, 50, 56, 62, 63, 64, 65, 71, 83, 84, 110, 115, 125, 126, 127, 128, 140, 144, 147*
Strong orb, *49*
Symmetry, *12, 16, 94, 112, 136, 145*
Symmetry Axis, *88, 94, 112, 136, 145, 147*
Terry, Gisele, *4*
Transits, *90, 113, 137*
Trine, *3, 40, 41, 47, 50, 59, 62, 63, 64, 71, 83, 84, 96, 109, 115, 125, 126, 127, 140, 144*
Triple Isotrap, *99*
T-Square, *54, 55, 60, 65, 128*
Unaspected planets, *52*
Unidecile, *61*
Witte, Alfred, *2*
Yod, *54, 55, 65, 128, 148*

Copyright © The Avalon School of Astrology, Inc. All Rights Reserved
All chart wheels and reports used in this module are created from Sirius 3.0 with permission from Cosmic Patterns Software.

Made in the USA
Coppell, TX
14 October 2022